MEMOIR IN TWO VOICES

MEMOIR IN TWO VOICES

FRANÇOIS MITTERRAND

ELIE WIESEL

TRANSLATED FROM THE FRENCH BY
RICHARD SEAVER AND TIMOTHY BENT

ARCADE PUBLISHING • NEW YORK

FIRST ENGLISH-LANGUAGE EDITION

Originally published in France under the title *Mémoire à deux voix*

Library of Congress Cataloging-in-Publication Data

Mitterrand, François, 1916–1996
[Mémoire à deux voix. English]
Memoir in two voices / François Mitterrand, Elie Wiesel.
p. cm.
ISBN 1-55970-338-5
1. Mitterrand, François, 1916–1996—Interviews. 2. Wiesel, Elie, 1928– —Interviews. 3. Presidents—France—Biography. 4. Authors, French—20th century—Biography. I. Wiesel, Elie, 1928– . II. Title.
DC423. M564 1996
944.083'8'092—dc20 95-53369

Published in the United States by Arcade Publishing, Inc., New York

Distributed by Little, Brown and Company

10 9 8 7 6 5 4 3 2 1

BP

Designed by API

PRINTED IN THE UNITED STATES OF AMERICA

For Lucia

Contents

I	CHILDHOOD	1
II	FAITH	37
III	WAR	93
IV	WRITING AND LITERATURE	129
V	POWER	153
VI	SPECIAL MOMENTS	171

Preface

A politician expresses himself first and foremost by his deeds; it is for them that he is ultimately responsible; speeches and writings are no more than supporting documents, secondary to the deeds themselves.

But when one's political career has drawn to a close, when one's lifework approaches an end, and with age the horizon moves ever closer, the need to take stock, to gather one's scattered thoughts into some sort of cohesive whole and put them into written form, becomes ever more compelling.

My life having reached the point it has — the end of my second term as president of France — I too now feel the need to express, in words too long suppressed, my deepest thoughts and feelings on a variety of subjects.

Such is the goal of the present book.

That is why I chose Elie Wiesel, a man I have known and respected for many years and with whom I knew I could speak openly and freely, to join me in formulating this memoir — a memoir, as it turned out, in two voices.

— François Mitterrand

I

CHILDHOOD

Elie Wiesel: For us Jews, the beginning is a basic necessity. The beginning preoccupies us more than the end. As the great German Jewish essayist Walter Benjamin put it, we dive into the future backward. Speaking personally, I look for myself in the past: it's the child within me who often determines my course of action. I would almost go so far as to say that it judges me. Is he — meaning the child — happy now? Was he in the past? These are the kinds of questions I ask myself. Let's begin at the beginning. What kind of childhood did you have?

François Mitterrand: My childhood, which was a happy one, illuminated my life. My parents were caring and open-minded. They did not hover over me or lean heavily on me. Nor did they impose any sort of blind authority as I was growing up. What they did instill in me, however, was a sense of discipline about life. Ours was a large family — eight children, plus two first cousins who were brought up as part of the family. Yet I was not lost in a caravan of noisy children. I could, if I so desired — and I did because that was my nature — carve out moments of solitude.

Until I was fourteen, I spent all my summer vacations in the country with my grandparents, in a house situated on a hillside overlooking a vast countryside, one and a half miles from the nearest village. The house was forty miles from Jarnac, right where the two administrative districts, the Dordogne and the Charente, meet, separated by the lovely little Dronne river. It was there that I came in contact, and filled my mind and heart, with the beauties of Nature: the wind, the air, the water; the ways and byways of the back country; the animals.

These experiences provided me, even at that early age, with a kind of philosophy. I was already able to sense that in the rocks and stones of the paths I trod there was a hidden energy. I had a profound awareness of, and deep relationship with, Nature. I went from one amazing discovery to another.

In those early years I can't remember ever once being hurt or offended by my elders, much less mistreated. Since I was born in the midst of World War I, in 1916, I have no memory of that bloody conflict, nor any scars. Hope — not regret or pain — was the sign under which I grew up. In a word, the real danger of those early years was that I would end up too much of an angel, seeing nothing but good in other people. But when I was nine, I was sent off to boarding school in Angouleme and came home only once every three months, at the end of each term. That added a dose of harsh reality to my youth: up at six in the morning and, in winter, I remember always being cold. Cold day in and day out. Yet I was fascinated by school; I was interested in everything. To be sure, I had a sense that there had been a basic change in my life, but that did not pose any problem for me. It was simply a new phase of my life, the basic structure of which remained unchanged.

Elie Wiesel: In my little village, which in winter was blanketed in snow, the Jewish children got up early, very early, to go to school — the *heder* — to say their morning prayers and study the Bible and the textual commentaries on the Scripture. During the winter I lighted my way with an oil lamp. It was dark outside, and I was afraid. The early part of my childhood was more or less that: fear of anti-Semitic thugs, fear of demons, fear of God. What about you? When did your childhood begin?

François Mitterrand: I was four or five when I first became aware of the world around me. My relationship with the world was immediate and direct, free of the "screen" that people, prejudice, and time imposed later on in life. The world was as young as I was. My head was filled with the music of Nature: the wind that was capable of giving you a good smack; the music of the mountain streams. Each hour had its own odor. Mine was a sensory life in those early days.

Children have a great gift of imagination. If I've had a fair share of original ideas in my adult life, none can compare in force and intensity to those I had when I was fifteen. The universe was seen and filtered through my own microcosm. Without knowing the world, I nonetheless dominated it. From that I evolved the notion of becoming preeminent in something, though what that might be I had no idea.

I spent a great deal of my youth with my maternal grandparents. As for my parents, they paid me occasional visits at school, and we were of course together during summer vacations.

Elie Wiesel: Did you ever have the feeling they were neglecting you? That they were abandoning you?

François Mitterrand: Not in the least! I simply saw that between their work and raising the rest of the children they had their hands full.

Elie Wiesel: My parents were also always busy. They worked from morning till night in the store. Prior to the high Holy Days, we children were expected to pitch in and give them a hand. In general, I saw my father on Thursday, the day I went with him to the synagogue. I was proud to be his son. As the quasi-official mediator of the community, he felt it his steadfast duty to serve it to the best of his ability. He obtained documents and authorizations for the needy; did whatever needed to be done to get people out of prison. But Saturdays he was home. Therefore, mine. I can't say I was close to him in those days, though; that came later on, when we were in the concentration camp together. When I was a child I thought I was closer to my friends than to my parents. What about you? Did you have friends when you were growing up? As for me, I tried to buy friends by offering them fruits and candies. I had a deep-rooted need to have friends.

François Mitterrand: I didn't have any real friends my own age except when I got to boarding school, and I must say I didn't mind not having any. I didn't really like the children of my family's friends. My family didn't socialize all that much when I was a child. Neither my parents nor my grandparents ever invited their friends over except for Sunday lunch. And besides, I was shy. I would never have taken the first step with someone I didn't know. When I was in the lycée — in second form as I recall — one of my teachers introduced me to the literary magazine NRF — the *Nouvelle revue française* — which was an exciting magazine in those days. My old friend Claude Roy, who like me was from Jarnac and who was a student at the Angouleme Lycée, used to spend hours heatedly discussing with me each issue's contents. Thanks to this wonderful writer, I entered the enchanted world where style ruled supreme. His literary knowledge and tastes were far in advance of mine; in fact, I'm still in the process of discovering today, in his books, a music that is his and his alone.

Elie Wiesel: Did you ever aspire to become a great writer?

François Mitterrand: If I had had one ambition, that would have been it. But I saw myself rather in the role of a popular orator at the Revolutionary Convention of 1792; if I was a writer, it was as the author of speeches at that historic assembly.

Elie Wiesel: As a child you didn't have any real friends and only rarely saw your parents? Whom did you turn to when you were unhappy or upset?

François Mitterrand: No one. I took long walks in the country. I went up into the attic. I gazed out at the countryside. I harangued an invisible public. I have a very clear memory of all that. The country around Touvent inspired me, and since I read in those days everything I could lay my hands on relating to the orators of the Revolution — the 1789 Revolution as well as that of 1848 — I was no doubt in a state of exaltation. From there, from this attic filled to the rafters with corn husks, standing at the little window that looked out onto the garden, I made my various appeals to History, modifying my speeches to suit my preference of the moment.

Elie Wiesel: I know the feeling. Whenever I hear music I feel as if I want to direct some invisible orchestra. What upset you as a child or made you suffer?

François Mitterrand: Injustice. Unfairness. Bias. It really bothered me when I felt I wasn't being understood. For example, I was by nature absentminded. But when I was accused of daydreaming, of being "out of it" — an accusation leveled at me fairly frequently — I was furious. My pride was hurt. I was also ambitious. When I was a student in Paris I dreamed of all sorts of adventures. I didn't think in terms of politics, but in a certain way I pictured myself in a position of power. Paradoxically, I was also attracted by the idea of a quiet life, a life of study and contemplation. My desires crisscrossed all over the place. I aspired to emulate the writers of the day. I was enamored of the word, of writing, whatever the mode of expression. And yet, again paradoxically, I was never garrulous. People said that I was an introvert, that I had trouble communicating with others. Actually, I've never been one to confide much in others. If people spoke ironically about my complicated, and no doubt contradictory, nature, I was touched. At school, there was one incident of gross injustice that absolutely infuriated me. I'm not one to carry grudges, but that painful memory remained with me for years.

Elie Wiesel: Are you still as withdrawn, still as shy today as you were then?

François Mitterrand: Yes, I am indeed.

Elie Wiesel: That's something adults are incapable of understanding: that children are proud, they have their own sense of self-respect. When you were a child, did you ever have moments of rebellion? Children always rebel against someone or something — their mother, their father, against adults in general, against the inevitable . . .

François Mitterrand: I never did, at least in the way you put it.

Elie Wiesel: Never? No rebellion whatsoever?

François Mitterrand: I had what you might call "sensitivities," but they were stippled revolts, fleeting moods.

Elie Wiesel: Were you ever sulky?

François Mitterrand: Sulky, no; sensitive, yes. Whenever I was offended by something said about me, or when I felt I was misjudged, I tended to react by clamming up. But that was all. I never rebelled. I didn't need to, at least at that stage of my life. What was there to rebel against?

Elie Wiesel: Being sent to bed without your supper, being told you couldn't read such and such a book.

François Mitterrand: No, not really. In our house there were no regulations. No one laid down any hard and fast rules. We had a tremendous amount of freedom, of latitude within the context of a strict family environment. Each Sunday we all attended mass. I learned Latin from the village priest. At Touvent, after mass, there was an obligatory lunch. But in fact family obligations took very little of our time. At mealtime we were fifteen or sixteen around the table, including my parents. It wouldn't even have occurred to us not to be there. Sometimes one child or another would show up late; my father strongly disapproved of these tardy arrivals, but he would say nothing.

Still, we could tell by the look on his face that he was displeased. And in the evening, if we wanted to read, play cards, listen to music, or even play table soccer, no one ever stopped us or told us it was time to go to bed. Mine was a middle-class family, lower middle class probably, but with a fair degree of independent thinking. I never felt the need to rebel against it.

Elie Wiesel: Were you mischievous as a child?

François Mitterrand: Not in the least. I was well-behaved as a child, fairly withdrawn. Not mischievous, but I did tend to poke fun at people. But I was not what you might call happy-go-lucky.

Elie Wiesel: A dreamer?

François Mitterrand: Yes. When you're part of a large family you have to find a way to be by yourself at times, to create what I might call "zones of solitude."

Elie Wiesel: And in these "zones of solitude" what did you do? What did you fill them with?

François Mitterrand: Reading. Or I would simply daydream, while away the hours, watch the shifting shades of light, both daylight and dark. I was fascinated by the way light alters the way things look, what it brings to and takes away from the world. In and of itself, light suffices to give the theater of childhood appearances that are amazingly different with each passing hour. Just the way shadows evolve and change on a wall, for instance. One could write a whole story about them.

Elie Wiesel: When you were young, did you write any poems?

François Mitterrand: Yes. The way most people do.

Elie Wiesel: Love poems? Meditative poems?

François Mitterrand: I was interested in words, in writing in general, in all its various forms. I was fascinated by and attuned to the world around me.

Elie Wiesel: You mean to Nature?

François Mitterrand: Yes, Nature above all. The love poems came later, when I was eighteen.

Elie Wiesel: Not before?

François Mitterrand: No. On the contrary, I flattered myself that I could write poetry in the classic mode, on subjects about which I was completely ignorant, inspired by the great writers of the seventeenth and nineteenth centuries.

Elie Wiesel: At this point were you an adolescent, or younger?

François Mitterrand: Younger. I was inspired by a particular place or view of the countryside more than anything else. I had a pronounced predilection for rivers and streams. So I made up my mind that every time I came to a body of water I'd write a poem to celebrate it. I never kept that promise! Early on, my goals were modest. I wrote about the rivers in my immediate vicinity: the Charente, the Seudre, the Gironde. As time went on and I traveled farther afield, I wrote about the Rhine, the

Rhone, the Garonne, then the Nile and the Niger. . . . Some of these poems still exist, and from time to time I enjoy rereading them.

Elie Wiesel: Why were you so fascinated by water? Why not the wind?

François Mitterrand: I think because I was moved and inspired by water, the thought of it flowing through continents, through all sorts of different landscapes until it emptied into the sea: for me that movement symbolized fate, evoked all kinds of symbols in my fledgling poet's mind.

Elie Wiesel: Needless to say, a psychoanalyst would surely have a field day interpreting that penchant.

François Mitterrand: You think so? Maybe you're right. But I've never been psychoanalyzed.

Elie Wiesel: Neither have I.

François Mitterrand: So I've never had the chance to have my innermost thought analyzed and interpreted.

Elie Wiesel: Let's come back to your family. Around that large family table you described, who did you feel closest to?

François Mitterrand: Among my siblings?

Elie Wiesel: Your siblings, or your mother or father.

François Mitterrand: Including my mother or father? I really can't say. We were such a closely knit, homogenous group. Besides, as I've said, from the time I was nine, maybe nine and a half, I didn't spend much time in the bosom of my family. I was at boarding school till I was seventeen. My mother died when I was nineteen. Since my father survived her by ten years, I knew him better than I knew my mother. I reached manhood while he was still alive, so I could understand him better.

Elie Wiesel: Children have trouble pinpointing the exact moment when they cease to be children. Can you tell me when, in your view, one becomes an adolescent?

François Mitterrand: I think it varies greatly from person to person. But I can say that, for myself, when I was fourteen a number of events occurred that clearly marked the end of my childhood: my grandparents' property was sold; I had to face the fact of death for the first time; and I moved into the upper school — all these events had an enormous impact on me. I had always somehow assumed that our close family would last forever. But it fell apart very quickly. In the short space of six years I lost my grandmother, my mother, and my grandfather. I never repudiated or disowned my childhood. Yet when I finished my secondary studies at the age of seventeen and moved to Paris, another phase of my life began. Naturally, I was no longer a child at that point; my eyes were opened to all sorts of new things, I became interested in adult problems, my reading habits changed.

Elie Wiesel: You had a happy — in any case uneventful — childhood. You say that by the time you were fifteen you were an adult. Yet in my experience people try to hang on to their childhood as long as possible.

François Mitterrand: When you grow up in the country I think you tend to mature more quickly. The cycle of the seasons, the timeless quality of life close to the earth, to Nature, make it easier for children to mature. The great upheaval was the war. That was when I learned the meaning of violence, of filth, of poverty, of the way crowds act or react. . . .

Elie Wiesel: Did you experience any "break," any rupture, as it were, between your childhood and adolescence?

François Mitterrand: No, not within myself.

Elie Wiesel: So for you the transition was a normal evolution.

François Mitterrand: I never broke away from anything, or experienced any palpable rupture, but there was, as I said, a major change when I left my Angouleme school and started my studies of law and political science in Paris. When I entered my tiny, ugly student room in Paris I didn't think, *I'm here to conquer Paris.* On the contrary, I felt lost, a tiny figure at the base of a mountain I was going to have to scale. I was without identity.

Elie Wiesel: In our house we were never allowed to refer to our father in the third person singular when he was there. Never "he" or "him"; we had to refer to him as Father. The father is father, not a stranger.

François Mitterrand: The notion of "stranger" begins once you leave the family circle. At our house, since we were not terribly social, guests were viewed to some degree as if they were guilty of breaking and entering, almost as burglars. We looked upon them with a mixture of curiosity and suspicion. That's why when I got to Paris I was suddenly thrust into a world that was indifferent, into living conditions that were tough, into a solitude that forced me to gird myself up for battle in a way I never had before.

Elie Wiesel: But up until this point there had not been any rebellion on your part? Not even an inner rebellion?

François Mitterrand: None, not even an inner rebellion.

Elie Wiesel: Against injustice?

François Mitterrand: Oh, yes. If you're referring to the outside world, I did participate in a number of the events of the period when I felt some gross injustice had taken place. And of course we students talked a great deal among ourselves about these things. But, I repeat, if you're talking about my immediate family, nothing.

Elie Wiesel: Your family, with whom you felt a close bond; your family, which you held sacrosanct.

François Mitterrand: Absolutely. As you can see, I'm not very original.

Elie Wiesel: On the contrary, you are. Most young people revolt almost as a matter of principle. In the old days, children were sacrificed to the gods. Jewish history begins with the failed sacrifice of Isaac. That's one of the most disturbing passages of the Scripture. It completely reflects the destiny of the Jews. I often think of that when I'm writing about events I've witnessed or participated in. Isaac's childhood is to some extent mine as well. Is one powerless as a child?

François Mitterrand: I think of childhood as a time of strength. When I was a child I felt I could do anything if I wanted to badly enough. That was my philosophy. When I need strength I draw on my childhood more than on any other source.

Elie Wiesel: As one grows older, one thinks more and more often, and more and more intensely, about one's own childhood.

François Mitterrand: That's true. Perhaps that's a constant, inevitable phenomenon as you grow older and feel death approaching. You go back to your origins, to your first emotions, your earliest feelings. I note that I'm more interested in poring over photographs of my childhood and adolescence than I ever was before. I spend hours looking at pictures of my parents and their friends, of the places where we lived. I love collecting pictures of that era, and when somebody presents me with some new ones I study them with great care, trying to figure out, through them, what I might have missed at the time. I discover a world I thought I knew. I also go back more and more frequently to the town of Saintonge, in the Charente province where I was born, and take endless walks there. Even though I haven't lived there for a long time, I still feel a real connection to the area. And the fact is, as a result of my long walks through the countryside I've ended up knowing the towns and villages of the region better now than I did when I used to live there. It's as if a distance — an interior distance — had kept me from getting to know it better when I was young. I used to ride my bicycle there, or crisscross the region in the back of my father's battered old car, and neither of these modes of transportation enabled me to seize and appreciate the beauty and quiet grace of the region as have my recent walks. I don't feel nostalgic about the place, but it does sadden me. For I know that this past, which I feel so strongly within me, will be swallowed up by the darkness as time goes by and will disappear completely after I'm gone. After my death, who will ever know or care about how I felt when I was with my parents and my grandparents, the emotions I experienced in my childhood home, my native village?

Elie Wiesel: What's become of your childhood home, the house you were born in and where you grew up?

François Mitterrand: After my father died it was passed on to us children in joint possession. As you may remember, we were eight children in all. As often happens, each of us took it for granted that one of the brothers or sisters would take care of it, which simply wasn't the case, and after several years we came to the realization that if nothing was done the house was going to fall into rack and ruin. So we decided to give it to one of our sisters, who now lives there part of the year. She has very little money, and the rest of that generation — my siblings — is collectively not very well off either, and as a result not much has been done over the years to keep the house in good repair. Thus it looks very much today as it always did; and there is the same musty odor when you step inside, a mixture of dust and humidity and saltpeter, of wood and plaster. And the garden smells the same, too. Proust said it better than I ever could, but these smells bring back a flood of powerful memories and emotions in me whenever I go back there. The house is still alive, packed with untouched memories. There is the room where I was born, where all my brothers and sisters were born, too — with one exception, a brother who was born in Angouleme.

Whenever it was time for one of us to come into this world, the midwife who lived across the street would come over to help my mother. Then the family doctor would be called, a man named Jules Hubert, I remember, a good and decent man who was totally bald. Whenever I go back there, I find my house exactly as it was. I think there are very few such places in the world, where things have remained virtually the same while so much else has changed so quickly, and so radically.

Elie Wiesel: I too find myself dwelling more and more on my childhood. But in my case it's not the same, because of the life I've led. I'm drawn inexorably back to the sites of my childhood. I've gone back three times to Sighet, and each time I haven't been able to stay; not only did I have to leave, but I felt I had to get away as soon as possible.

François Mitterrand: You have a burden of memory different from mine, because you were uprooted from your birthplace. You lived a life of exile, finding a new home in a new land. Exiled from your childhood, or at least from your youth; first from Hungary, then there was the war, the deportations, the concentration camp. In my case, until the age of twenty-two my life was stable. My early memories remained intact; there were no superimposed memories to alter or deform them.

Elie Wiesel: We're all exiles in a way. From the time you are taken from your mother's womb; then you move away from your family, from the places where you spent your youth; then from memory itself.

François Mitterrand: I know. Like snakes, we shed our successive skins.

Elie Wiesel: I remember that when I arrived back at my birthplace I had the impression I didn't recognize either the city or the house we had lived in. And yet the house was still standing, right where it had always been. But there were strangers living in it.

François Mitterrand: Where was this?

Elie Wiesel: At Sighet. It used to be part of Rumania, then became part of Hungary. It was the same place, but the name had changed.

François Mitterrand: And after two or three days you felt you had to leave?

Elie Wiesel: After a few *hours.*

François Mitterrand: A few hours . . . Were you bored?

Elie Wiesel: No, no. I was suddenly overwhelmed with anxiety, as if I had arrived in a hostile country. I had to get away as soon as I possibly could. Flee. To somewhere, anywhere, but in any case not remain there for another minute. The following day I took the plane back home to the United States.

François Mitterrand: That was because you had lost . . . It's unbearable.

Elie Wiesel: It was because nothing had changed. The furniture was there; the door still made the same sound when it opened.

François Mitterrand: Your house belonged to other people now.

Elie Wiesel: Yes. People I didn't know, people who had never laid eyes on me before and hadn't the faintest notion who I was.

François Mitterrand: I have the same feeling sometimes — with less intensity I'm sure — when I go back to Touvent.

Elie Wiesel: Does it ever happen that you see yourself again as a child?

François Mitterrand: Yes, sometimes. Images float to the surface. I see myself climbing a sloping hill; I see a stream, a cluster of trees, with me resting at the foot of one of them. There I remade the world. These perceptions of childhood, even if they're not precise, remain a precious refuge.

Elie Wiesel: We cherish our childhood, we keep coming back to it again and again. We judge it, just as it judges us. What do you say today to the child you were?

François Mitterrand: I have nothing to say to it inwardly.

Elie Wiesel: There's no dialogue between you?

François Mitterrand: Not really. Nothing meaningful, in any event.

Elie Wiesel: And yet literature is a dialogue between adult and child. As is philosophy.

François Mitterrand: You may be right. I sense that there exists within me an immutable place where the child I was —

with its character, its nature, its personality — has not changed. It occupies a relatively small surface in the context of my total being, of course, but its value remains important. And besides, everything around it has changed in the intervening years. But the little diamond has remained intact.

Elie Wiesel: It's an anchor?

François Mitterrand: Exactly. And if I were to accept your notion of a dialogue between me and my childhood — which I don't feel personally — I would say that in my case it serves as a point of reference. I have the impression that what I possessed at that point of my life, or what little of it remains (and there's no doubt that something does), represents the purest and most limpid portion of my personality.

Elie Wiesel: For me, that dialogue does exist. A dialogue between the child within me and the adult it became. Sometimes I feel that the child accompanies me, questions me, judges me.

François Mitterrand: I completely understand what you're saying. I see very clearly the foibles and failures of my later life in relationship to the dreams, the demands of childhood. From that viewpoint, my childhood is indeed my judge. But let's not be overly dramatic. More than anything else, I have a sense of the continuity of my life from childhood on.

Elie Wiesel: When a child comes into this world it is born with all the nuances possible. It has its demands, its ambitions. The child within me has created me. What about you?

François Mitterrand: As I said before, I had greater intuitive powers when I was fifteen than I have today. I had a sense of the transience of life, borne out by what I experienced later. At this stage of my life, my sensory perceptions, what really matters to me, are rooted in my childhood passions. The child I was determines my impressions and my judgment, not my deeds.

Elie Wiesel: Doesn't he influence you any more than that?

François Mitterrand: He's a point of reference, no more, no less. Whenever I find myself in a difficult situation, all I need to do is recall what I already sensed.

Elie Wiesel: Still, it's the child who asks you: "So, Adult, what have you done with my future?"

François Mitterrand: Before we come face to face with the real world we are extremely demanding. For ourselves and for others as well.

Elie Wiesel: Which is wonderful, is it not? One doesn't lie to children; we don't have the right to lie to children. It's too big a betrayal. Today, I'm like putty in the hands of a child. I can cry, I can laugh, I'm happy or miserable simply because a child looks at me or I look at a child. And whenever I try to illustrate something tragic, or explain the human condition today, I always refer to children. Whatever I've done in the area of human rights has always been done with children in mind. I see the photograph of a child in tears, the children of Biafra or, today, the children of the former Yugoslavia. I'm sure you saw the photograph of, or read about, the 120 retarded children who two or three years ago were taken thirty miles outside Sarajevo and abandoned there.

François Mitterrand: Yes, I know, it's painful beyond belief. Unbearable.

Elie Wiesel: Intolerable! When I heard about those children I said to myself: If only I'd been closer to you, Mr. President — closer geographically, I mean — I would have advised you to dispatch some planes immediately to pick those children up and bring them back here — those poor abandoned children, hungry and thirsty and completely alone in the middle of nowhere, 120 grimy, unwashed children, physically and mentally ill, who had been given up even by their nurses, who had allowed them to be taken out to die. What can one do today, in the world we live in, to protect childen who cannot fend for themselves?

François Mitterrand: Make ourselves constantly and acutely aware of the problem.

Elie Wiesel: Awareness, yes. But how do we turn that awareness into concrete, positive action?

François Mitterrand: Do as much as you can within the context of your power and authority.

Elie Wiesel: Is that an admission of impotence?

François Mitterrand: Rather an admission that the case you cite is part and parcel of the world's misfortune. Which is not to say that I've resigned myself to fatalism, but the fact remains, we have still not evolved beyond the barbaric stage of evolution. We see that taking place here and now, before our very eyes.

Elie Wiesel: It's as if the world today is incapable of coexisting with these children.

François Mitterrand: I think you have a view of the world . . .

Elie Wiesel: . . . that's overly idealistic. Perhaps.

François Mitterrand: Romantic, almost mystic, no? The feelings you express are not common currency today. I think we all bear within us a portion of barbarism. Life moves on without the slightest regard for human beings, young or old, who are crushed like so many ants on a log.

Elie Wiesel: Which means that people are paying the price so that we can move forward. We kill children, kill childhood, so that man can move on and attain adulthood.

François Mitterrand: I'm not sure I quite agree with that.

Elie Wiesel: Today it's Sarajevo. Sarajevo is all but finished. Everywhere I go I hear people saying: "Poor Sarajevo! What can we do to help poor Sarajevo?"

François Mitterrand: It's true that that city, so long under siege in a region dominated by the Bosnian Serbs, is terribly vulnerable. Even in the various plans set forth for specifying distinct areas for the Bosnian Serbs, Croats, and Muslims, no one has mapped out a corridor allowing that city to be integrated into the Muslim bloc. But today the United Nations forces are still firmly there, and the Bosnian Serbs would be taking a monumental risk if they tried to overrun the UN forces and capture the city. To do so they would have to leave the bodies of United Nations soldiers in their wake, with all the repercussions that would entail. On the other hand, one hesitates to think what might happen if the UN forces ever withdrew.

Elie Wiesel: The Bosnian Serb forces have possession of the hills overlooking Sarajevo, which opens the way for them to take Sarajevo itself.

François Mitterrand: "Opens the way" is a very vague phrase. The Serbs have been occupying the hills surrounding Sarajevo for a very long time. They can see exactly what's going on in the city. And virtually all the suburbs are in the hands of the Serbs.

Elie Wiesel: I'm afraid . . . I'm afraid of what will happen when and if they capture the city itself. There's every reason to believe that terrible atrocities will be committed if they gain control. I wonder if some sort of gesture can't be made.

François Mitterrand: What kind of gesture? We already have several thousand soldiers stationed there under the banner of the United Nations.

Elie Wiesel: Let me ask you a question. Assuming the Serbs do take Sarajevo, what about your rallying, say, fifty or so intellectuals to go there and simply be present when the Serbs arrive. As witnesses, to save human lives. I'm sure we would save lives simply by our presence.

François Mitterrand: That's an idea a number of people have bandied about.

Elie Wiesel: If you decide to act upon it, it goes without saying that you can count on me to be part of the group. But let's go back to our subject of conversation, namely childhood. I'm a firm believer in the mystery of childhood. What about you?

François Mitterrand: No. The mystery of life remains complete: it's the break of day, the first light. But the child as such is not mysterious.

Elie Wiesel: A child's life is mysterious.

François Mitterrand: Life . . . We come into this world, we grow up, we go on, we age, we disappear. Nature's round and rhythm, as it has always been. The only thing is, when you come into this world you are a pristine being, knowing nothing. Certain genes handed down to you from preceding generations have perhaps prepared you for life, but everything is to be learned, every feeling and emotion is to be experienced. A person's first sensations are so strong they dominate the rest of his life, simply because they are the first he's experienced. They impress themselves on virgin canvas.

Elie Wiesel: One Talmudic scholar compares the child to a blank piece of paper — which will make psychologists howl with rage. But that's nonetheless true. It is the beginning, the mystery of the beginning. Before, there is nothing. And on this nothingness, everything is inscribed, and this void becomes something that exists, that unfolds and blossoms.

François Mitterrand: But that state, that pristine period, does not last very long in any case.

Elie Wiesel: Yes, but what about life itself?

François Mitterrand: Childhood is a fleeting stage of life. Moreover, there are actually several childhoods. If you look at a newborn child, remind yourself that in three months or six months this child will not be the same person, not only physically but morally and intellectually as well. Later, in two or three years, the child will crystallize, but that child too will change and be different three or four years later. Whenever you look at a child, you always have to tell yourself that you will know this child for only a brief moment in time, no more, for when you look again another child will have taken his place. We are always seeing a child for the last time.

Elie Wiesel: My references are almost without exception religious in nature. Perhaps because, when I was a child, religion played such an important part in my life. Did you have a religious upbringing?

François Mitterrand: All the members of my family were practicing Catholics.

Elie Wiesel: Did you serve at mass?

François Mitterrand: Yes, of course.

Elie Wiesel: With General Bénouville?[1]

François Mitterrand: We must have served mass together, since we were classmates at Angouleme. As for my parents, my father came from a long line of devout Catholics. On my

---

[1] Pierre de Bénouville was a childhood friend of François Mitterrand's who later served in the Resistance under the name "Lahire."

mother's side, going back to my maternal grandfather, he and his parents before him belonged to the upper middle class, which was rationalist, so their return to the fold was more recent. But my mother herself, and her mother before her, were both devout, deeply committed Catholics. That was the climate I grew up in.

Elie Wiesel: Was that an enriching experience, or were you a churchgoer because your family was?

François Mitterrand: It was enriching. There are mystical values — impressions of music, of songs and religious chants, an odor specific to churches, a combination of incense and lilies (of course, there are other flowers, too, but lilies are the one I remember), which create an intense poetry. Whenever I walk into the Jarnac church, as I recently did to check on the renovations being made there, I am immediately assailed by that odor, which is the same as when I was a child.

Elie Wiesel: For me that same odor spelled fear. Whenever I passed a church and caught a whiff of that odor, I crossed the street. Each of us has to cope with his early memories, of course. Have you ever noticed that all religions focus on children: the Christ child, Moses as a baby, the childhood of Buddha? Is there a message to be learned from the fact that each religious founder seems to emphasize childhood?

François Mitterrand: I presume because childhood is the time of innocence, of purity, the time of authenticity. It's as you were saying a little while ago: the beginning. The desire to begin, to go back and begin again, over and over again, is a powerful element in any religion.

Elie Wiesel: And also because religions, in my view, appeal to a state of innocence; that is, to childhood.

François Mitterrand: The focus also stems from the fact that religions are well aware that during youth our minds are most impressionable.

Elie Wiesel: There is a strange declaration in the Talmud. It says that since the destruction of the Temple of Jerusalem, prophets and the gift of prophecy no longer exist; prophetic gifts, it maintains, are the exclusive realm of madmen and children.

François Mitterrand: Yes, I'm aware of that. Children, and those deemed mad, are not bound by reason. And as you well know, religions require faith, and faith implies an element of the irrational.

Elie Wiesel: Children are free. Free to reason beyond reason, as it were.

François Mitterrand: Precisely.

Elie Wiesel: For personal reasons, I also equate childhood with illness. I was sickly as a child. My mother took me to see some of the most eminent Hasidic masters, to be blessed by them, and she also took me to see some of the most famous doctors of the day. If I was able to visit Budapest, it was because the doctors sent me there to be examined by some renowned specialist or another. In my view, the real break with childhood takes place with the awareness or intrusion of death into a child's life. A child in mourning is no longer a child. Did death ever intrude in your life when you were young?

François Mitterrand: Yes, several times, though not in my immediate family. As I said, we were not raised in a cocoon; I was free to come and go as I pleased. My only restriction was that I was forbidden to set foot in the local stream until I had learned how to swim. But my brothers and I discovered a spot in the stream where we could wade across, which goes to show that I wasn't a very obedient child. The first time I came face to face with death must have been when I was twelve. It was the month of June. One of my classmates, a black boy named Alphonse, was balking at going into the water. Finally he did, and it turned out that he didn't know how to swim and drowned immediately. I was a hundred or so yards away when it happened, so I didn't actually see him drown, but I was there when they removed his body from the water. I didn't go to the funeral because I didn't know Alphonse's parents. But his death, and those of several other classmates, had a profound effect on me. Yet for a long time thereafter I still felt I was immortal! Immortal's a big word. So while other people's deaths did affect me, I still felt that I was destined to live a long life. Even during the war, when faced with the imminent threat of death, I wasn't afraid. Except perhaps the first day, when I was up in the front lines and the Germans let loose an artillery barrage against our positions. The first time that happened I was deeply impressed; I had a physical reaction that doubtless was fear. I didn't think I was going to die, but my body, all my senses, reacted. Courage isn't the absence of fear; it's being able to dominate your fear.

Elie Wiesel: Do you remember the first time you were in mourning? I can recall very clearly the burial of one of my cousins, the candles burning at the head of her casket, my aunt's tears, the whispered voices of the mourners. I also remember the death of a Hasidic master. All the shops in the area were closed in mourning. As his funeral procession passed through the streets, people lined the route, sobbing.

François Mitterrand: Between the two wars, during the economic crisis of 1929–30, my grandparents sold their Touvent property. That was my first period of mourning. A real mourning, as if I had lost a beloved friend. I remember being in the house when the movers began taking the furniture out. In the corner of one of the rooms my grandmother was sitting in an easy chair, her eyes red from crying, and I was there next to her, in a state of total despair.

Not long after the sale of the property, my grandmother died. I think it's safe to say that that marked the end of my childood. Of course, one might say that I was lucky not to have encountered death any earlier in my young life.

When my grandmother died, I just sat there for hours as if I had been turned into stone, crying my heart out. I would have deemed it a betrayal to have left the room where my grandmother was lying. Death isn't simply a momentary separation. I didn't take my eyes off her till they closed the casket. She was well along in years, seventy-five in fact. My relationship with her was a very special one. I knew that she loved me simply and profoundly.

She died one night in August, during our summer vacation. My parents didn't want us children to stay with her, but as soon as I heard she had died I went into her room anyway and, as I said, stayed there till the funeral.

Elie Wiesel: Did you cry at the funeral?

François Mitterrand: I've always had trouble expressing my feelings, especially in public. But when I was alone with her, of course I cried. Her death marked the first loss among those who were really close to me, people I loved. I wasn't thinking of death in general when my grandmother died, I was thinking of *her* death. I felt very close to her. Before she died, my grandmother had called for me. They were her last words. I was totally overcome, and what made me even sadder was the thought that one day my sorrow would be less acute. I thought that time and the demands of life would make me forget, and that that would be a betrayal of her, of the bonds between us.

Elie Wiesel: When someone dies, we are summoned by his or her death. The terrible mystery of death. The Angel of Death is described as the "emissary of the living." They say that he is covered with eyes; when he casts a glance in your direction, he kills. Death is the look of the living.

François Mitterrand: I think of it as an eternal separation.

Elie Wiesel: Even though Catholics believe that they will be reunited with their loved ones in another world?

François Mitterrand: As far as I'm concerned, death is forever. I tell myself that while we're of this world, we the living have to remain faithful to the dead. I often swear to myself that I won't let a day go by without remembering the departed. And for the most part I've kept my word. Every evening I devote a certain amount of time to reflection. I make a point of remembering all those who were close to me at one point of my life or another, even those with whom I was not close emotionally. I always had the feeling that my memory would be a well-tended graveyard. To think of the dead is to ensure the survival of those you've loved, while waiting for others to do the same for you later on. It's a duty of memory. I see myself as the guardian of the door to a fortress — the guardian of memory. My grandmother's name was Eugenie. She was born during the Second Empire.[2] I felt responsible for keeping her memory alive; I was the witness to her life.

Elie Wiesel: Did she have a happy life?

François Mitterrand: She had four children. Her oldest son died when he was still a child. Her second son died of galloping consumption when he was twenty. Those two deaths almost destroyed her.

Elie Wiesel: Did she transfer her love to you?

François Mitterrand: I think so. She made no bones about the fact that she had a special affection for me. My grandfather was a very colorful man, with opinions on every subject under the sun. He lived until he was eighty-five. I was twenty when he died, and by then I was hardened to the realities of life. I was deeply affected by his death, but given his age it was easier to accept.

---

[2] The Second Empire was founded following Louis-Napoléon's coup d'état in 1852 and lasted until France's defeat in 1870.

Elie Wiesel: My grandmother lived with us in Sighet, so I knew her. But I never knew my paternal grandfather, who had been a stretcher bearer in World War I and was killed in action. Several years ago I paid a visit to the cemetery in our village and I found his tombstone. I saw that his name was the same as mine.

François Mitterrand: We don't have that tradition, which I find a lovely one. This said, on the Mitterrand family tree there are several "Gilberts" from the sixteenth century on.

Elie Wiesel: We can trace our names back to Abraham and David. When enemies waged war against us, they were also waging war against our names. They understood that names are the source of memory.

François Mitterrand: True. My father's first name was Jules, which was the first name of a long line of famous Frenchmen.

Elie Wiesel: What are your memories of your mother's death?

François Mitterrand: My mother died five years after my grandmother. I was home at the time. My mother suffered from a heart condition, and for the last two years of her life she was for all intents and purposes an invalid. During her last year she was bedridden. My siblings and I took turns sitting at her bedside. She was in a coma the last three days of her life, so there was not really a precise or discernible "moment" when she died.

Elie Wiesel: Was the pain of your mother's death as intense as that of your grandmother's?

François Mitterrand: Yes, with the difference that in my mother's case I was expecting it. For me the greatest pain was that hers was such a lingering death.

II

FAITH

Elie Wiesel: As a child, you were a devout Catholic. In fact, your secondary schooling was under the tutelage of Catholic priests.

François Mitterrand: Not exactly. Our school, unlike those run by the Jesuits, where religious philosophy and theory dominate, was a diocesan secondary school. The teachers at Saint-Paul of Angouleme were secular priests for the most part, and some of them were peasant-priests. So while it was nominally Catholic, religious teaching and rigor were not as overwhelming as in Jesuit schools.

Elie Wiesel: All I meant was that for you, as for me, from very early on in your life faith played an important if not a central role.

François Mitterrand: No, not really. I had the faith that was taught me both at home and at school. And by temperament I think it safe to say that I have a religious bent. I'm interested in the kinds of questions religions pose. I'm naturally inclined to ponder these questions within myself. Fundamentally, I admit the existence of a principle, and of an explanation, but my mind falters at the forms of the explanation. That basic notion greatly influenced my education. Natural inclination leads me to be interested in the study of these problems as well as in the various works that focus on them. I like their literary forms as well as their stylistic expression. All of which would lead people to draw the same conclusion you did about my faith. In fact, I'm an agnostic. I don't know whether I know; I don't know whether I *don't* know. Which cannot fairly be termed "faith."

Elie Wiesel: And yet, at some point you said, recalling your childhood, "Time and things all bespoke God with great clarity."

François Mitterrand: That's true. I felt that kind of certainty. But I was expressing that as an idea, a principle — in order to avoid using the word *God* — that governs and ordains. And in all fairness I would say that, in the context of my agnosticism, if I lean in one direction it's on the side of faith. Yet I have to add that I am not a practicing Catholic. What is more, I mistrust all dogmas.

Elie Wiesel: I think that one can revolt against God. Sometimes, the only way a believer can express his faith is to reject, or at least question, it.

François Mitterrand: I didn't rebel against God. I never made the gesture of tearing up any religious ID card, or formally leaving a church. I never cut any religious umbilical cord. Little by little over the years I took a certain distance, and that evolution took place within me, in acordance with the vicissitudes of life.

Elie Wiesel: So there was never any rupture, any drama so far as your faith was concerned, only a slow evolution. Do you remember the moment when you began to lose your faith?

François Mitterrand: Since I never experienced anything like Pascal's night — in other words, a moment of illumination when doubt overwhelmed blind faith — I obviously can't pinpoint such a moment. But I think it dates from World War II.

Elie Wiesel: I can remember the first time I failed to put on the phylacteries. It was in 1949, in Israel. I was with a journalist, and I was so terribly busy that day I simply forgot to put them on. For me it was terrible, because I was so devout. But the world did not collapse under my feet. And yet, I had been convinced that if I committed such an act I would be struck down on the spot.

François Mitterrand: But you did survive!

Elie Wiesel: Yes, because God is patient. Somewhere you said: "Freedom means breaking away."

François Mitterrand: Yes, that's always the case. First, from a practical viewpoint, freedom has to be earned. Freedom means passing from one state to another, tearing yourself away from something. In other words, breaking away. To take a personal example, when I was a prisoner of war and wanted to regain my freedom, I had to make up my mind, one early morning in March, that I was going to make a break with the prison camp routine and in so doing accept the consequences and risks that that decision entailed. When you cut the barbed wire hemming you in, that's making a conscious break with your previous condition. That image remains engraved in my mind. There are times, you know, when the loss of freedom can be comfortable, even in the worst of situations. That "comfort" comes quite naturally, within the context of an established order, even if that order is working against you. You have to prefer another "comfort," that of the mind unfettered, to impel you to make the break.

Elie Wiesel: A long time ago I spent a full year in the hospital because of a chronic circulatory problem I was suffering from. Then one day the doctor came and said to me, "I'm releasing you from the hospital tomorrow." And instead of being overjoyed, I was actually afraid.

François Mitterrand: I understand that perfectly. To come back to the case I just mentioned, I almost changed my mind about escaping from the prison camp in March of 1941, because a few days earlier my family had sent me a package in which there was, among other things, a magnificent pair of boots. Since they were brand new, there was no way I could take them with me — they would have made me easy to spot. (All-points bulletin: "The escaped prisoner is wearing a new pair of boots.") Absurd as it seems, I was tempted to stay so that I wouldn't have to give up my boots!

Elie Wiesel: The freedom to *not* be free is, in a sense, a form of freedom.

François Mitterrand: In that case, however, one has to be free to choose. I had the choice of staying put. For me, the only real freedom was to come and go as I pleased, wherever I wanted; to go back to my country, pick up the battle where I had left off, renew old friendships — in short, cast off the state of servitude into which I had been forced. Of course, I also had the freedom to say, "I can go home again, but I prefer to stay." I had a friend whose name was Antoine Mauduit. An admirable man. He was deported to Bergen-Belsen, and after he was liberated he stayed on at the camp for several days to help care for the other inmates, refusing the offer made to him by the authorities to take the first train back. I remember waiting for him with his wife at the train station in Paris, only to learn from the returning deportees of his decision to stay. He caught typhus fever and died from it a short while later. That is freedom in its highest form, the freedom of sacrifice.

Elie Wiesel: Or, another way of putting it, freedom transformed into faith.

François Mitterrand: Precisely. For him, who had converted to Catholicism and had not only a deep, abiding faith but a sense of saintliness, it *was* faith. The only way he knew how to act was in the absolute.

Elie Wiesel: What was he before he converted?

François Mitterrand: I'm not quite sure what his earlier religious beliefs were. I do know that he was a nonbeliever; until that day, before the war, when he had a revelation, an illumination. From a very wealthy family, he became a migrant worker, moving from job to job as the seasons dictated. He joined the Foreign Legion, to break completely with his past life. He fought as a legionnaire in World War II, was taken prisoner; then, under circumstances that escape me, was repatriated. At that point he founded a kind of phalanstery high up in the Alps, a kind of religious community open to people of all beliefs who could find comfort and security together. Until one day he was arrested and deported to Bergen-Belsen.

Elie Wiesel: Camus once asked whether one could become a saint without believing in God.

François Mitterrand: I think the answer is yes. God is a spur, an incentive, a motivation superior to any other. Certain laymen and laywomen, who were nonbelievers, experienced the most arid of sainthoods; their reference was a way of being, an individual morality, a set of personal ethics, and their only reward was the feeling that they had accomplished their own mission.

Elie Wiesel: It sounds strikingly like the communists.

François Mitterrand: Faith is transformed into dogma, and no matter what camp you choose, you can be dogmatic. So the communists have had their saints and heroes who, out of belief in or respect for the dogma of communism, have sacrificed themselves, even unto martyrdom.

Elie Wiesel: The communist vocabulary is a religious if not mystical vocabulary, and there is no question in my mind that communism considers itself a religion. There was Marx and Lenin, and then all the others, who were its prophets.

François Mitterrand: You're absolutely right. Any religion generally tries to control every aspect of a person's life, leaving nothing to chance. The language, the mind, everything one says and does is enrolled in the service of communist ideology. On that score, you'll note that the Catholic countries of southern Europe were ultimately the places where communism made the deepest inroads, where the largest portion of our society of practicing Catholics made the transition to militant communists. And while that transition was doubtless painful and difficult for many who made it, the essential nature of the matrix out of which they came remained the same.

Elie Wiesel: Do you truly believe that faith is necessarily and inevitably linked to dogmas? Don't you think that faith can exist without dogma?

François Mitterrand: I said that solely in the context of the communists. Putting aside for the moment those rare human beings whom I would call exceptional or extraordinary, most people need their faith to be nourished, to be sustained. And for that the common mortal needs to buttress his or her faith by surrounding it with a set of key ideas or beliefs, of rituals and procedures. Therein lies the role of churches, which produce their dogmas. When one is a believer, to have no church requires an extraordinary act of heroism, an individual adventure of the mind and spirit that is extremely difficult.

Elie Wiesel: Can one, must one, have faith even as one searches for faith? For Christians, is it always a gift, a sort of grace?

François Mitterrand: "You would not be searching for me if you hadn't already found me," said Pascal. One continues to search for faith even after one has already found it. Any number of accounts bear witness to that fact. The great mystic Theresa of Avila for one; Theresa of Lisieux, the uneducated little nun, for another. Ultimately, the world's great mystics have spent half their lives plagued by doubts, even though in their heart of hearts their faith remains intact: I doubt, I am in the desert, God is absent, but I continue to believe in and serve Him.

Elie Wiesel: In other words, faith is a challenge.

François Mitterrand: If it's true faith, yes. Doubt inevitably goes hand in hand with faith. I'm not referring to those whose faith is lukewarm, who have it because it was given them and keep it handy more out of habit than belief.

Elie Wiesel: Mysticism interests you, doesn't it? I can tell it intrigues and attracts you. Can you tell me why?

François Mitterrand: We all have our moments of mysticism. But perhaps you're right. Why the attraction? Because of poetry. Mystics infuse both beings and things with a burst of poetry, however fleeting, and this suddenly makes me want to understand the world and existence in another way, not simply rationally and according to the laws of science.

Elie Wiesel: Do you still read books about mysticism?

François Mitterrand: Books about mystics, in any case. Theresa of Avila, Saint Francis of Assissi, Saint John of the Cross, even "Little Theresa," who I just mentioned, Theresa of the Christ child, an extraordinary personality. Books about them abound, and can be found in every library around the world.

Elie Wiesel: How about other religions? Do you ever read anything about Jewish traditions, about Sufism[3] or Buddhism?

---

[3] Refers to the movement inspired by the seventeenth-century Muslim mystic Sufi.

François Mitterrand: I can't say I really have. I know all the books of the Bible, Old Testament and New. But the Bible is not a very mystical document.

Elie Wiesel: The Bible serves as the foundation for the entire Jewish tradition. There are nonetheless a fair number of things that spring from the irrational.

François Mitterrand: I don't think it's fair to say that everything irrational is of necessity mystical. The Bible is a book of reason, the handbook of an entire people.

Elie Wiesel: A while back you mentioned science as something opposed to faith. But doesn't a pure intelligence, which conceives of the universe as a category of ideas, require faith as well?

François Mitterrand: I can't say for sure if scientists need faith, but I can assert that many scholars in our Western societies do have faith, Christian faith. They accept the idea of miracle, they accept the Trinity, they accept the mysteries surrounding the birth of Jesus. Which proves that faith, when it takes hold of a mind or soul, is stronger than scientific reason. The greatest scientific minds, who as you say demand of their thought the absolute clarity of categories, are suddenly capable of taking a plunge. When scientists ponder their own fate, their own personal destiny, and come up with no reply, if they have faith they find therein the comfort they need.

Elie Wiesel: At Oxford and Harvard I have met a number of world-famous physicists who are not only fervent Catholics but believe in the theological dogma of the Church.

François Mitterrand: But if scientists have no faith, that's quite another kettle of fish. There are eminent scholars and renowned intellectuals whose faith came to them through science; for others, on the contrary, science alienated them from faith.

Elie Wiesel: One day some NASA scientists invited me to give a lecture on mysticism. I must say the invitation took me aback, but I nonetheless accepted. I asked them why people like themselves, who were completely focused on science, on space, were interested in hearing my ideas on mysticism. Their answer was that, having reached the limits of knowledge, they were interested in exploring what lay beyond. In their view, if faith did exist, it could only be of a mystical nature.

François Mitterrand: Ask any of the greatest scientists of our time and they will all tell you that the human mind still does not have an answer to the question "why"; the responses to the question "how" are countless. Between the most subtle, the most up-to-date "how" as it relates to the most daring discovery today — whether it be in the realm of mathematics, biology, or astronomy — and the "why" are light-years. And yet we know that today's "how" will rapidly be overtaken by another "how," which will in turn — even as I speak — be succeeded by still another. Nature does not change. I therefore believe that we have no choice but to take the plunge. The most rigorous, the most analytic of minds must, at a certain moment in his life, make a leap of faith — of childlike faith, as Christ was wont to say.

Elie Wiesel: "Why," in other words, must be the question of questions. Why did God create the world? Why does the world exist?

François Mitterrand: The beginning of the world. We have accumulated a mountain of "hows" without making the slightest dent on the ultimate question, "Why?" We talk about quarks, about black holes, and we could well spend the next several thousand years gaining new scientific insights into just how the universe began without finding the explanation of why.

Elie Wiesel: Which brings us back to mysticism, the mystery of the beginning.

François Mitterrand: In the beginning was the Word.

Elie Wiesel: Not for the Jews. *Bereshit Bara:* "In the beginning God created Heaven and Earth. . . ." With the Word. But what was there before the Word?

François Mitterrand: If I had the answer then I would have faith.

Elie Wiesel: And my opinion is exactly the opposite. If you knew the answer, you would not have faith.

François Mitterrand: In any case, I would have certitude. If I were to look for the explanation using purely materialistic reasoning, I would be right to have faith in something other than knowledge of the mechanisms. It seems to me that there has to be something that gets the machine going. Voltaire said as much in his fable of the clockmaker.

Elie Wiesel: What are the traps of faith?

François Mitterrand: The most obvious trap is that of self-satisfaction, by which I mean looking no further, pushing on no farther in one's spiritual odyssey. Obscurantism derives from that. Galileo became anathema, or the alchemists; any new experiment, any new scientific discovery, was witchcraft, to be cast out and condemned.

Elie Wiesel: An approach to life that has a name: fanaticism.

François Mitterrand: Precisely. Faith — or more properly, dogmatism — leads to sectarianism, intolerance, therefore persecution. Man's basic instincts take over. We persecute and at the same time strengthen our hold on power. The surest way any religion has of perpetuating its teaching, its faith, is to maintain its position of power. History is filled with examples of this basic truth.

Elie Wiesel: Religions should never allow themselves to slip into fanaticism. Yet so many do, as history shows all too well. Faith — I mean profound, complete faith — and tolerance seem to be mutually incompatible.

François Mitterrand: Not to my mind. But I have to confess that every passing day offers more evidence that you are right. People possessed of what I might term "tolerant faith" are indeed few and far between. Such people so ardently desire that the world be ruled and regulated according to the dictates that govern their own lives.

Elie Wiesel: Mystics, whatever their religious beliefs, seem to be in a special category. It would appear that they have a kind of basic understanding among themselves.

François Mitterrand: Because they are in another world.

Elie Wiesel: There are differences among Christians, Jews, and Muslims, yet only in appearances. Mystics come together, as it were, find a common ground, in the "other world" to which you referred. But there are differences, which cause faith to spill over into fanaticism.

François Mitterrand: It may well be that some religions have given birth to tolerant faiths, but for the life of me I can't think of one. To be sure, there are some men who were able, because of their education or life experiences, to reconcile faith and tolerance: Saint Francis of Assissi, for one. But far more often, faith has given rise to those whose militant rallying cry is: "Death to the Infidel!"

Elie Wiesel: Not only is militancy still prevalent today, it is increasing. Does the rise in fundamentalism we've been witnessing over the past several years concern you?

François Mitterrand: It not only concerns me, it disgusts me. Without wanting to resort to immoderate terms, I nonetheless believe that fundamentalists are basically stupid. What revelation have they received? Who has annointed them to be the ultimate judge, with the power to punish, to attack, to . . .

Elie Wiesel: . . . to kill? Today, fundamentalists are killing people in Algeria, in Iran. Fanaticism is blind, it renders its adherents deaf and blind.

François Mitterrand: In my view, fanaticism is without exception an act of stupidity. I find it totally detestable. Quite simply, it is one of the most dangerous evils confronting the human race.

Elie Wiesel: Because it denies the right of inquiry and therefore negates culture.

François Mitterrand: Because it denies life.

Elie Wiesel: The fanatic does not question anything. He suffers no pangs of doubt. He knows, he thinks he knows.

François Mitterrand: Doubt is useful.

Elie Wiesel: Yes, but only when it impels one to question. Which allows culture to flourish. How do you fight fanaticism?

François Mitterrand: By avoiding at all costs counter-fanaticism.

Elie Wiesel: You mean that an antifanaticist movement can be as dangerous as fanaticism itself.

François Mitterrand: Of course. There is a great temptation to fight fire with fire. That is, resort to the same means used by the fanatic movement one is opposing: the fanatic strikes with such and such a weapon; we'll strike back with one even more powerful. You have to respect your own laws, your own code of conduct, and not let yourself be caught up in the fanatics' own game, refuse to play by their rules. And you don't have much room in which to maneuver, because you cannot be weak. Wisdom, prudence, and resolution are the qualities you need in dealing with fanaticism of any stripe. For over half a century now, since the end of the fascist and Nazi ideologies, fanaticism and terrorism have not been able to make meaningful inroads into our Western societies.

Elie Wiesel: Who has been responsible for that? Or rather *what* has? Isn't educating people to the dangers of fanaticism the real answer? In fact, isn't education the only remedy?

François Mitterrand: Education is certainly one remedy, but it's not the only one. Remember that Pic de la Mirandola was one of Savonarola's most fanatic partisans.[4] He comes off as one of the great humanists of his time, yet when his mentor called for him to burn books he did so without a moment's hesitation.

Elie Wiesel: He was also the disciple of a great Jewish philosopher and mystic, Abraham Aboulefia. You mentioned a while ago that in your opinion one could be a saint without having faith. Which leads me to ask another question: can one be a layperson, even an agnostic, and have faith?

François Mitterrand: The terms are semantically incompatible. Agnosticism by its very definition implies the absence of faith.

Elie Wiesel: What I meant was, can one's faith in humanity and one's faith in God be compatible?

---

[4] Fra Girolamo Savonarola (1452–1498), a monk who started a popular movement against corruption and worldly excess that, for a time, controlled Florence. He was later excommunicated and executed as a heretic.

François Mitterrand: By all means. There are many people whose faith in humanity is made all the stronger by the fact that they refuse to resort to any supernatural explanation. But it seems to me that humanity, as it frees itself increasingly from the fetters of the past, as its mind uncovers and encompasses new areas of knowledge and moves progressively forward, is the bearer of a message that transcends it. Faith in humanity and faith in God are not mutually exclusive; quite the contrary.

Elie Wiesel: The reason I ask is that some people have used their faith in humanity as a reason for challenging faith in God.

François Mitterrand: These two mind-sets can and do co-exist and quite often complement each other. But there is another viewpoint, which is that of people who, having placed their faith in mankind, believe it is more beautiful, more noble — given their belief that there is no afterlife — to live their lives in accordance with a certain set of ethics, a certain rigorous and demanding moral code.

Elie Wiesel: I knew François Mauriac[5] very well. He was almost in love with Jesus Christ. He was more interested in the person of Christ than he was in Christianity itself. Does the death of Jesus interest or intrigue you?

François Mitterrand: Very much so. He is someone who, in the eyes of His disciples, was both man and God at the same

---

[5] François Mauriac (1885–1970), novelist, poet, and educator, was a friend of Mitterrand's mother. Mitterrand wrote a long review of Mauriac's novel *The Dark Angels* while a student. Mauriac won the Nobel Prize in 1952.

time. How can that be? From the earliest Christian times, people have wrestled with the question of whether Christ was more man than God or more God than man. Various Christian sects have not only argued that question over the centuries but have massacred one another mercilessly over it.

Elie Wiesel: Isn't it possible to think that all humanity consists of both man and God in varying degrees?

François Mitterrand: From the mystical viewpoint, without question. For in the eyes of Christians, all men were created in the image of God. And to accept that notion clearly implies that in each of us there is a reflection of God, and in some people more than a reflection.

Elie Wiesel: What would have happened if Jesus had died a natural death?

François Mitterrand: There would have been no message to the world. Christ died to serve mankind.

Elie Wiesel: In other words, He took upon Himself the suffering of humanity.

François Mitterrand: Not only that, He *died* for humanity. Without which the mission would not have been accomplished.

Elie Wiesel: Do you think it's possible to suffer for another person?

François Mitterrand: That is the very idea that lies at the heart of Jesus' life and death.

Elie Wiesel: Do you believe in the idea?

François Mitterrand: I have read virtually everything that has been written on the subject. Historically, I believe that Christ did exist. And I believe that a man can accept to fulfill such a role. Let's say it lies within the realm of human possibility. Whether they be saints or heroes, we know of enough cases of exceptional people who did knowingly die for the good of humanity.

Elie Wiesel: I can conceive that Jesus believed in that notion, and that His followers did as well. But personally, as a Jew, I don't understand. For us, it is impossible to suffer *for* someone. I can suffer *with* someone, and perhaps even die with someone, but I can neither suffer nor die in his or her place.

François Mitterrand: Speaking for myself, I believe that Jesus' death was part and parcel of the message he was entrusted to transmit to the world.

Elie Wiesel: In periods of stress, or when one is in a state of distress, one either moves closer to God or further away.

François Mitterrand: In most such cases, I believe people move closer to God. But to my mind that is not the noblest of motives for believing, for the simple reason that it is fear of the unknown that impels one rather than true belief. We are suddenly overwhelmed by all the fears accumulated since the world began, and so we seek refuge. As you say, there are cases when distress can cause one to turn away from God, too. For example, those who have been witness to terrible atrocities often turn their backs on God.

Elie Wiesel: During World War II I knew some people who, believers though they were until then, became atheists; and I knew others who were atheists and found faith. Napoléon once said, "You don't will yourself to become an atheist."

François Mitterrand: Why would one want to *will* oneself to become an atheist? I'm not sure I understand the point of such an effort.

Elie Wiesel: To revolt against authority. Communism in a sense represented an effort to free people from the so-called yoke of God.

François Mitterrand: Communism considered that religions were oppressive and also that they were the allies of the ruling powers. They taught that religions kept the masses from becoming educated and thinking for themselves. So your viewpoint is not without some foundation in fact. Since the communists themselves substituted one form of church for another, however, they can't exactly brag about their results. But to come back to what you were just saying, during the war I had a natural movement toward God, because all my reflexes pointed me in that direction, as did my education. Yet in all objectivity, that period and the period immediately following the war did not bring me closer to God. There were moments when I prayed, almost instinctively, and yet by the end of the war my skepticism was, if anything, greater than it had been before.

Elie Wiesel: Do you think your "faith" — that is, your agnosticism — can be passed on to anyone else?

François Mitterrand: Let's not talk about my faith. Like many people, I pose my share of questions, and, as I've said before, I have a certain natural tendency toward the spiritual. But I don't feel I'm in a position to discuss with you the basis — or nonbasis — of my faith. If you raise the subject of faith, all I can say is that I haven't enough of it to be in any position to communicate it.

Elie Wiesel: Even in the presence of a man of faith?

François Mitterrand: If such a person's deeds are in accordance with his principles, then I might well be not only impressed by him but affected in what I do and think.

Elie Wiesel: In the course of your life you have met several men of deep faith, haven't you? Several popes?

François Mitterrand: Men of profound faith, yes. Mauriac, Massignon, Mauduit, monks from the Sinai.[6] A Jesuit, Father Delobre — a number of others, including my father. And several popes, too: Pope Pius XII, John XXIII, Pope Paul VI. I never met Pope John Paul I, for he was pope for so short a time. The one I've seen most often is of course Pope John Paul II, since as president of France I was in a situation where I dealt with him directly in my official capacity.

Elie Wiesel: France is historically a largely Catholic country.

---

[6] Louis Massignon (1883–1962) was a professor at the College de France and a leading expert on Islamic mysticism. Antoine Mauduit, a friend of Mitterrand's, helped found an anti-German organization during the occupation.

That being so, what are the relations between Church and State? Is it a confrontational relationship?

François Mitterrand: Not really. Occasionally, when the Church makes up its mind to try to increase its power or influence in the realm of education, when it becomes worried about the role of religious education in our school system, frictions do arise. But all in all I don't really see it as a serious problem.

Elie Wiesel: You once said: "I understood the meaning of injustice when I read the Sermon on the Mount." Could you elaborate?

François Mitterrand: The Sermon on the Mount is one of the most beautiful texts I've ever read. Just think, Christ uttered those words roughly two thousand years ago, and basically nothing has changed. Christ could justify His return among us solely on the basis of giving the same speech. The only thing is, instead of going up on the mountain, where chances are there would be nobody to hear Him, He'd probably choose to talk in some ghetto.

Elie Wiesel: And how do you think He would be received?

François Mitterrand: In all likelihood, the bishop would lodge a complaint with the local mayor, who would ask the speaker to give his speech somewhere else.

Elie Wiesel: Do you ever ask yourself whether God is just or unjust? Isn't that really the story of Dostoyevski's Grand Inquisitor?

François Mitterrand: I constantly hear people declaring that God is just, and I keep wondering what the basis is for that assertion. I'm sure you've noticed that in sermons from the pulpit, funeral orations, or speeches given by the clergy in times of grave crisis, almost without exception the priest or minister or rabbi all voice their belief that God is just — and even good. I have a hard time reconciling that assertion with the catastrophes that abound in the world.

Elie Wiesel: Generally speaking, funeral orations are intended not for the deceased but for his or her family and close friends, to console them and make them feel better.

François Mitterrand: There are things in this world that I have learned, and there are things I would like to believe. And then there is what I actually see and know from personal experience. Nothing demonstrates convincingly to me the existence of a higher justice.

Elie Wiesel: Justice in the eyes of God, not in the eyes of man. Each time I wrestle with that question, I come to the conclusion that I just can't understand.

François Mitterrand: That's where I end up when I try as well. I'm not saying that God is unjust; I simply say, "I don't know whether God is just." I am of the opinion that the order of the world, or the disorder if you will, does not follow any law of justice, at least in the sense that we perceive it.

Elie Wiesel: What in your view would constitute justice?

François Mitterrand: That noble and generous acts be recognized as such and inspire others to emulate them, that acts of cruelty also be recognized and abhorred. But the fact is, so far as I've been able to see there is no difference between them in our day-to-day lives. Isn't it possible that in the conscience of those who commit a good or noble act there is a feeling of joy or even pleasure on the one hand, or perhaps a twinge of sadness on the other for not acting as they might have? That is called having a conscience. Not everyone has a conscience, and even those who do or think they do are prone to lapses.

Elie Wiesel: If someone is punished, he or she is not alone in being punished. Children, family, endure it as well. We do not suffer alone. We always suffer with those who suffer because of our suffering. But to come back to the subject of injustice, I know you well enough to say that whenever and wherever you perceive it you try to do something about it.

François Mitterrand: I think I can say without fear of appearing immodest that my reflexes and my reflection incline in that direction. I cannot bear injustice. I may be far from perfect, but my abhorrence of injustice is unqualified.

Elie Wiesel: When you come right down to it, isn't what remains of a man's life his struggle to eradicate injustice?

François Mitterrand: That is without doubt one of the noblest battles one can wage. It has guided my political choices, and I continue to believe that I was right. But in addition to the element of injustice that led me to act, there came, as time went on, the burning desire to verbalize it. For awareness of injustice in and of itself is not enough to combat it. To make people aware not only of injustice itself but of its consequences requires one to analyze society almost scientifically. Why do injustices occur? Generally speaking, they emanate from the class struggle, the belief or conviction that one segment of society is repressing another. Plus the thirst for power. In other words, injustice stems from the age-old law of the jungle, the survival of the fittest.

Elie Wiesel: Have you been been unjust toward someone?

François Mitterrand: Probably, but I can say in all fairness that I have never been willingly unjust. It happened when I was simply in a foul mood, or hadn't given sufficient thought to the consequences of my decisions.

Elie Wiesel: When you become aware of it, what do you do?

François Mitterrand: I try to repair the injustice, and if I can't for one reason or another it upsets me, at least for a time.

Elie Wiesel: For me, the worst injustice is humiliation. Whenever I see someone being humiliated, my impulse is to react, to protest.

François Mitterrand: I feel the same way. I'm sure there have been times in my life and career when I have humiliated people. They'll forgive me when they realize that I didn't do it on purpose. In any event, to humiliate reveals a lack of self-control, a lack of education.

Elie Wiesel: Have you ever been humiliated? During the war, when you were taken prisoner by the Germans, did you feel humiliated by having lost the war?

François Mitterrand: Not at all. That is, I didn't feel personally humiliated. But angry, yes; I joined in the collective anger, the feeling of national humiliation.

Elie Wiesel: In your heart of hearts you were still carrying on the fight.

François Mitterrand: Exactly. I never thought the war was lost. I say that to give you a general impression I had at the time; that conclusion was not the result of any historical analysis. I simply thought that yesterday's mistake would be rectified tomorrow.

Elie Wiesel: Would it be fair to say that this same notion applies to Christ? That He lives in the present but His death is timeless?

François Mitterrand: When it comes to explaining why Christ was condemned to death and crucified, you have to take into account the local conditions of the time and place.

Elie Wiesel: The Romans were responsible?

François Mitterrand: No, they carefully refrained from getting involved. Basically it was an internecine struggle between Jews: the eternal struggle between entrenched orthodoxy, consecrated by both religious dogma and hierarchy, and what is called heresy — a deviation from accepted doctrine.

Elie Wiesel: In ancient Greece, heresy meant doubt, and later on was punishable by death.

François Mitterrand: In any case, insofar as the death of Jesus is concerned, I've never read anything that would lead me to believe differently.

Elie Wiesel: But Renan[7] is not an authority on Jewish questions.

François Mitterrand: Renan viewed the Jews as an Arab tribe. I can see that that doesn't sit well with you. Why? Renan contributed greatly to getting the issues out on the table. Besides, nonbelievers through the years have related that story and come to the same conclusion I have: that Christ was a serious thorn in the side of the Jewish religious hierarchy. And what happened then, in Christ's day, found a clear echo in Christianity itself from the third through the eighteenth centuries, in the way the Church dealt with its own heretics. You may recall that in the eighteenth century a nineteen-year-old aristocrat, Chevalier Jean-François Lefebvre de la Barre, was sentenced to death and executed. His crime was not having doffed his hat when the Holy Sacrament passed by, and it was further reported that he also had had a sarcastic smile on his face. The Church authorities duly noted that, compounding his sin, not only was there a broken cross on one of the town bridges but, to make matters even worse, a group of young men had been heard singing songs of a dubious nature. As a result they first cut out the chevalier's tongue, then shaved his head and cut it off. But that does not suffice to condemn the entire Church; I have no doubt that many priests who are aware of that crime deplore it fully as much as I do. The fault lies with the Church hierarchy, who will go to any lengths to enforce their dogma. Which leads me back to the seemingly inevitable conclusion that the Jewish

---

[7] Ernest Renan (1823–1892) was the author, most famously, of *The Life of Jesus* (1863), which lost him his professorship in Hebrew at the College de France.

hierarchy of the day viewed Jesus as a serious embarrassment. And following the crucifixion of Jesus, many of his disciples were put to death as well: James, Philip, Stephen, all of whom spelled trouble for orthodox Jews.

Elie Wiesel: Still, the prophet Jeremiah was a far sharper thorn in the side of orthodoxy than Jesus ever was, and yet they never sentenced him to death.

François Mitterrand: Of all the prophets in the Old Testament, Jeremiah is the one I find least attractive. He's a loudmouth, and a whiny one to boot; he's a bit of a collaborator, and overly ambitious. Which is why I'm always surprised when any of my friends name their children Jeremiah, even if the name does have a nice ring to it.

Elie Wiesel: I must say I respectfully disagree with you. I think you're being overly harsh toward Jeremiah. First of all, he never aspired to be king. In fact, he didn't even want to be a prophet, poor man. I feel sorry for him. And his language was so incredibly beautiful, almost as beautiful as Isaiah's. At some point later on I'm going to try to rehabilitate Jeremiah in your eyes. But I'd like to come back to Dostoyevski. He once wrote: "If God does not exist, then anything goes." Do you agree with that statement?

François Mitterrand: No. He's dead wrong. At the very least, God is an important source of help for the way many people lead their lives; and even if He weren't, Dostoyevski is still wrong.

Elie Wiesel: What bothers me about Dostoyevski is the

ubiquity of God in his work. God is everywhere, on the side of the vanquished as well as on the side of the victors; He is with those who suffer and with those who inflict the suffering. Think of the priests on both sides who bless their respective armies on the eve of their setting off to massacre each other; it's not as if they were doing battle to prove that the earth didn't revolve about the sun, after all! All this said, I'm sure it's fair to presume that faith, for those who feel the need of it, constitutes an important bulwark against absurdity.

François Mitterrand: I'm not one of those who go about proclaiming that faith is absurd. That would be a giant step toward the affirmation of a counterfaith.

Elie Wiesel: People are afraid of the absurd.

François Mitterrand: Yet you would have to be incredibly vain to think that you could lead your life relying only on your own resources. Besides, think of the element of hope that faith implies. Transcendence carries with it the whole, very potent element of hope.

Elie Wiesel: Speaking of which, did you pray when you were young?

François Mitterrand: Of course I did. Sincerely, profoundly.

Elie Wiesel: And do you sometimes still feel the need to pray?

François Mitterrand: Occasionally. But in my own way. I don't focus on anything in particular. Or on anyone. I think that we all need to pray; that is, to seek communication through thought. One of the loveliest aspects of the Catholic Church is the Communion of Saints, which when you come down to it is the community of prayer, and that goes back to early esoteric rites. The fact of praying here, at this spot, while you know that a thousand miles away, at precisely the same moment, someone else is offering up the same prayer, and that that same phenomenon is being repeated countless times around the world, is in essence establishing a communion of souls among all those far-flung people. At the risk of sounding simplistic, given how airwaves can carry both sound and image worldwide, what makes us think that these same waves can't transmit a great intensity of thought? That notion doesn't strike me as all that absurd; in any event, it's a lovely idea. In all honesty, if I do on occasion pray — not in the narrow sense of the term but in the true sense — I don't set myself up as a man more detached from his fate than he really is.

Elie Wiesel: When was the last time you prayed?

François Mitterrand: I'd be hard pressed to say. That all depends on how you define prayer. If you mean directing your thought toward a superior — and ultimately unknown or unknowable — being, that is something I do quite often. That may not strike you as very reasonable, but, very simply, both my education and my nature incline me in that direction. But before I've gone on very long, my reason tends to step in and break off the dialogue, which may actually be only a monologue.

Elie Wiesel: Does God need prayer?

François Mitterrand: You're talking like a true believer!

Elie Wiesel: The fact is I do situate myself within the parameters of faith.

François Mitterrand: Not I. If it's a question of reciting words I've learned by heart to solicit divine intervention, to communicate with a transcendental world, then the answer is "yes," there are times when I pray, I do repeat the words that are engraved in my mind; I repeat them out of habit, education, sometimes even out of need. But I do not pray as a man of faith, with the feeling that I'm communicating or that my prayers are being heard or answered.

Elie Wiesel: Traditionally, there are two kinds of prayers: those in which the communicant solicits and those in which he or she gives thanks. One still has first to believe.

François Mitterrand: In my experience we tend to ask for help or protection in times of need and to forget to give thanks when we're happy. All of which strikes me as highly suspect.

Elie Wiesel: When you were told about your present illness, or later when you were being prepared for the operating room, did you pray?

François Mitterrand: I'm no more courageous than the next person! I knew I was dealing with something serious, even life-threatening. But in my heart of hearts I didn't really believe it. At the time of the operation, therefore, I was completely at peace. I willed myself to be an object. There are times in life — when you're in an accident, for example — when you somehow manage to look at yourself as if you're not the main character in the drama that is unfolding.

Elie Wiesel: I saw you on September 10, 1992, the evening before your first operation. When I think back to that meeting, I'm dumbfounded. You seemed so completely detached. Never could I have imagined . . .

François Mitterrand: I'm not a great one for sharing my innermost thoughts or secrets. Besides, I thought that even if it was important to me personally, in the larger scheme of things it was banal, innocuous. To be sure, I can't say I was looking forward to the operation. I have a low threshold of pain; I turn my head away when I get an injection or a blood test — which is to say that I don't get up in the morning thirsty to play the role of a hero. But once the die are cast, I can handle the situation. I'm a resigned patient. Imagined pain or suffering is unbearable; when it's real you almost always learn how to cope with it.

Elie Wiesel: That's exactly what those who have been tortured maintain: the anticipation of torture is worse than the torture itself. That has always frightened me. I have no idea whether or not I would refuse to talk if I were being subjected to torture.

François Mitterrand: People of our generation have without exception had to ask themselves that question, and no one has had the courage to say with any degree of certainty: "I could hold out."

Elie Wiesel: In an interview you granted where the subject was your illness, you made a reference to the late Arthur Ashe. You said that when you learned of your illness your first reaction was to ask: "Why me?" That seems to be the normal reaction. I remember that when I first learned I had been awarded the Nobel Peace Prize my immediate reaction was the same: "Why me?" That question nagged me for the rest of the day. "Why me?" Was I more worthy, more deserving than others? Certainly not. Then my mind flashed back several decades to Buchenwald, to April 1945. The Germans had begun to evacuate the camp. On more than one occasion I had found myself standing only a step or two away from the main iron gate. Beyond it lay the voyage toward death. But the quotas had all been filled. Who was the person or persons who had gone through that gate before me, perhaps in my stead? This same thought kept crossing my mind the day of the Nobel Prize ceremonies in Stockholm.

François Mitterrand: You can chalk that up to luck. Life is an extraordinary game of chance, a real lottery. Why does one number come up rather than another?

Elie Wiesel: Do you know the work of Nikos Kazantzakis, the author of *Zorba the Greek* and *Christ Recrucified*? You may recall that in one of his books he quotes this very lovely Etruscan proverb: "It's not because two clouds meet that lightning flashes; two clouds meet so that lightning will flash." I believe that the mystery resides in the fact of meeting. I've always been moved by your interest in the Jewish people.

François Mitterrand: The history of the Jewish people and the message they bring to the world make it virtually mandatory to be interested in them. But let's not exaggerate my role. I behave toward the Jewish people the way I believe to be proper, useful, and fair: by helping them get justice. No more. Speaking personally, I see in them and in their history influences that are very important to me. Doesn't the civilization I live in today have its roots in Jewish history? And who isn't interested in going back to explore their roots?

Elie Wiesel: Of all the peoples of antiquity, the Jews are the only ones to have survived. How do you explain that?

François Mitterrand: You're forgetting China and India. But if by antiquity you're limiting your perspective to Greece and Persia, then of course you're right. How to explain the survival of the Jewish people? Doubtless because of their relatively small numbers. Great empires, great masses of people, have a hard time maintaining their true identity. I think that the methods used by the leading lights — those who best expressed the soul of the Jewish people — were less idealistic than realistic. Just look at the Bible. It's the book that encompasses the wants and aspirations not simply of an individual or a family but of an entire people. It just so happens that the Jewish people were also held together by a common set of beliefs, a religion that inspired the monotheistic religions that have come down to us today, and that Jewish familes or communities, wherever the diaspora might have landed them, held firmly to this set of beliefs, which was a way for them to hold onto their past. To be sure, people who believe in the God of Israel will add that they are God's chosen people, and that God watches over them.

Elie Wiesel: A collective mission and vocation.

François Mitterrand: That is a theological explanation, but there are others. As for myself, I don't hold to the former; that is, the theological explanation. I believe that it's far easier for a persecuted people to survive when they are relatively few in number. First, there was the period when Jews settled in this or that country, wherever they could. Only much later was there a single state, two actually, though one of them soon disappeared. As for the other, though it still did exist, it was subservient to Syria. Despite all the persecutions and deportations they have suffered through the ages, despite being scattered from one end of the globe to the other, the Jewish people have managed to survive. Their power of resilience, severely tested, has forged their soul.

Elie Wiesel: I have always been amazed that so tiny a people, without any territorial ambition except that of claiming what is theirs, has survived.

François Mitterrand: That is why I have always felt that whenever Israel moved to expand beyond its own natural borders — whether to the Golan Heights, the Sinai, or Lebanon — it was making a mistake, committing a historical error. It is true that the situation of modern Israel is highly ambiguous: most of the territory that Israel occupies today belongs to Jewish history. But the international community of nations fails to recognize the heart of its history: Jerusalem, the kingdom of Judea, a good part of the ancient royal kingdom of Israel.

Elie Wiesel: You have almost vindicated certain choices that Israel made without going outside its biblical boundaries.

François Mitterrand: I even seem to have remembered the only two passages in the Bible that seem to extrapolate, in words ascribed to God, the notion of a greater Israel.

Elie Wiesel: In other words, you understand Israel historically.

François Mitterrand: Yes, but I also understand the confusions attending its historical claims to the land. Because over the centuries the Arabs have settled there, set down roots that in many cases are now centuries deep, and made the land their own country. Whence arises the incredibly complicated situation we find ourselves in today: two prophets, two religions, two countries, and one piece of land.

Elie Wiesel: You have long been a proponent of giving the Palestinians a country they can call their own. But how on a practical level can you do it? The land is a minefield. But there is also a combination of such high hope on the one hand and deep distress on the other that one can only look toward the future with fear. Even granted that a peace treaty has been signed, the problems separating Arabs and Jews will not, it seems to me, be easily solved.

François Mitterrand: Two peoples, one piece of land: it will take a great deal of imaginative statesmanship to carve out a fair and acceptable federation. I take a certain pride in having long ago recommended the kind of partition that has now taken place. I am happy to have suggested it earlier enough on so that I feel at peace with what is taking place. Yasser Arafat visited me on two different occasions: the first time when he came as the head of the PLO, the second when he was part of a mission headed up by ex-president Jimmy Carter. Once when you and I were discussing Yasser Arafat, we talked of the confidence that was vested in the man. But in retrospect it wasn't really a question of confidence, it was a matter of facing the facts. You negotiate with those you've been fighting. You can't play games with History; and Israel, by wanting to deal with intermediaries it had itself chosen, was making a tactical mistake, in my view. That Israel had reproaches to make against its adversary — that is, against Arafat — goes without saying; otherwise he would not have been an adversary. Terrorism is tragic and inexcusable, but the real political force of the Arabs *was* the PLO, which was the only military representative of a country, a people at war, a people without a land. We had to face up to the fact that those political realities had to be dealt with.

Elie Wiesel: You're no doubt right, but you also must know that when you were talking with Yasser Arafat here in this very office, right outside in the hallway his aide Farouk Kadumi was telling your advisers that whatever the "old man" was telling you was so much garbage; the fact was, the rest of the PLO would settle for no less than all of Israel.

François Mitterrand: In any movement you'll find people who refuse to compromise. In fact, the present agreement between Israel and the PLO is on very shaky ground, because there are dangerous extremists on both sides who will settle for nothing less than total victory. But my fondest hope is that the two sides will achieve a stable peace. I have always said that one could not ask the Palestinians to go without a homeland. And in fact this tiny piece of land — Gaza, Jericho — possesses an extraordinary symbolic power.

Elie Wiesel: And what about the formula: "First Gaza and Jericho, then . . . ?"

François Mitterrand: That is being said in the context of the negotiations, of course. One side is saying: "That's all, and no more," and the other side is responding, "We won't settle for *only* that." And then a new discussion takes off from that point.

Elie Wiesel: You love Israel, you love that land. When you talk about it, you always do so with a great deal of emotion.

François Mitterrand: Until I went there for the first time in 1980, Jerusalem was in my eyes a place of myth. And when I was there, when I saw Jews living in this ancient land, when I saw Jerusalem, touched it, I was indeed deeply moved. For me, who thinks of himself as a student of history, it was an extraordinary time-warp.

Elie Wiesel: Would you like to spend some time in Jerusalem, living and writing there?

François Mitterrand: I'd love to write there. It's a spot of earth that awakens all sorts of desires in me. It's not the only such place on earth, of course, but it's a place in which so many elements — spiritual, intellectual, historical, and political — come together, as nowhere else on earth. So with the burdens of office no longer mine, I would love to spend some time there, stroll through its streets, let my mind wander through the labyrinths of history, visit the holy places, meet some of the city's intellectual and religious leaders.

Elie Wiesel: A photographer mentioned to me one day that Jerusalem was an impossibly difficult city to photograph. Because of the light. He explained to me that light is measured in "luxes" and that one of the most beautiful sites for a photographer is the south of France, Provence, where the light measures sixteen luxes. After that, he said, there is Tibet, with twenty-four luxes. But in Jerusalem the light reaches thirty-six luxes; in other words, according to him, the brightest place in the world.

François Mitterrand: Throughout that region — and not only in Jerusalem — everything is intense. You're speaking only of Israel, but you must remember that throughout the ages all the peoples of the region were consumed by faith. Civil wars there are inevitably wars of religion. From one Lebanese village to the next people have been killing one another for centuries on end because of religious differences within the same religion. How many Christian sects are there in Lebanon? Six, seven, eight? And how many Muslim? Just about as many. And within these religions people fight with as much intensity as they do between two different religions. From time immemorial each religion or sect is imbued with the same fervor, burning with the same religious passion, as if each stone in that region were composed of explosive religious atoms. It's a land scorched by religious fervor.

Elie Wiesel: Did you know the major political leaders of Israel — Ben-Gurion, Golda Meir, Moshe Dayan?

François Mitterrand: I never met Ben-Gurion, but I knew Golda Meir quite well. Before I became president, I went to see her several times in Israel, and she came to see me in Paris. We also corresponded a number of times. She was working very hard to help Russian Jews emigrate to Israel, and I served as an intermediary for her. It was a very tricky business, one that required enormous discretion, but we did have our fair share of successes. I also saw Begin fairly often before he became prime minister, and admired him greatly. But I think he made a major mistake with the war against Lebanon. As for Moshe Dayan, yes, I knew him very well. Whenever I went to Jerusalem, whether he was in power or not, I always paid him a visit. So, yes, I knew them all personally, including Igal Alon, a wonderful man.

Elie Wiesel: People talk about the Jewish "mystery"; do you believe in the mystery of Jewish existence?

François Mitterrand: I don't quite see what the mystery might be. It's more a matter of an exception, an example of extraordinary vitality. A tiny tribe emerged thirty-five hundred or four thousand years ago from Mesopotamia. One of its members, a powerful and gifted man, Abraham, encountered God and believed in Him. And that belief has continued down to today.

Elie Wiesel: We could easily have disappeared. In fact, I have sometimes wondered why at a certain point in time a council of elders wasn't convened to pass on the following message to God: "Listen, God, either You want us here below or You don't. Why don't You just leave us alone for a little while, so that we can live in peace. Otherwise, we'll have to believe You want a world without Jews."

François Mitterrand: If we're to believe the explanation of the Bible, God needs the Jewish people as much as the Jewish people need God. If the Jewish people were to disappear, they would be playing a nasty trick on God. In short, they hold to God.

Elie Wiesel: Without being aware of it, you are saying almost word for word what the Talmud says. In the Bible we find the following verse: "God says to the Jews: 'You are my witnesses.'" The Talmud adds: "And God says: 'If you are my witnesses, I am God; if you are not my witnesses, I am not God.'" A while ago you had harsh words for the prophet Jeremiah. Can you tell me why?

François Mitterrand: As I said earlier, he's an unseemly character, highly ambitious and not exactly straight in his relations with the Assyrians.

Elie Wiesel: But he's also the only person in the Bible to have foretold a catastrophe — namely the destruction of the Temple in the year 586 B.C.E. — and lived to tell about it. And instead of decamping to Assyria after the catastrophe — that is, to the Babylonians — who would have welcomed him with open arms because, as you rightly point out, he more or less collaborated with them — he went with the exiled Jews into Egypt. He strikes me as being the most tragic of all the Jewish prophets. And his writings are of a lyrical beauty almost unequaled in the Bible.

François Mitterrand: Jeremiah was a howler. At that time, people began to take on an apocalyptic tone. That Jeremiah foretold the coming destruction of the Temple may actually be a less amazing prophecy than you seem to think. It was increasingly clear that one was entering a period of decline. No, say what you will, I do not like Jeremiah. I much prefer Isaiah. His teaching is brilliant.

Elie Wiesel: They call him the Prince of Prophets. First because he is of royal blood; and also because his style, his use of language, is indeed princely. Which biblical character do you relate to most closely?

François Mitterrand: That's a difficult choice to make, because the Genesis is both history and legend. David is too complicated; no, he's not my model. Perhaps Saul.

Elie Wiesel: Saul did not aspire to be king; they forced it upon him, and he ended up a suicide. A victim of God, in a sense. I find myself drawn to him in a very profound way.

François Mitterrand: I'm sure we're almost instinctively drawn to the underdog, or to the person who has suffered. King Yannai[8] also strikes me as being an interesting character.

Elie Wiesel: What about Herodius?

François Mitterrand: He was a great king, but how by any stretch of the imagination do you make him a part of Jewish history? He wasn't Jewish.

Elie Wiesel: A descendant of the Edomites, he was a man of great violence. The cause of too many deaths. You have a profound knowledge of Jewish history, I see.

---

[8] Alexander Yannai (126–76 B.C.E.), a Hasmonean king, ruled Judea from 103–76 B.C.E., his reign marked by wars of conquest and internecine strife.

François Mitterrand: The Bible interests me deeply. It's a terrifying book with its massacres, a pitiless book. The Bible is a reflection of its time, which was a period of violence. But what strength in its pages, what poetry.

Elie Wiesel: It was written at a time when the country was being conquered. I, who delight in rehabilitating our ancestors, remember searching high and low in the Bible for a passage that would endow Joshua with at least a modicum of human warmth. And I finally found it: Joshua, who did conquer Israel and settle there, died in complete solitude. No one came to his funeral.

François Mitterrand: He died in disgrace, that's why. To come back to your earlier question, the biblical character I find most compelling — and please forgive the banality of the choice — is, after all, Moses.

Elie Wiesel: Joshua? Disgraced? I don't think so. For us he incarnates complete allegiance to Moses. He never left him. As for Moses himself, in James Joyce's *Ulysses,* there's an astonishing passage that has always stuck in my mind. It's the point where Moses, the Prince of Egypt, decides to leave the palace and rejoin his people. As he is taking his leave he meets the high priest, who says to him: "Moses, you're mad! You were Prince of Egypt. Today Egypt is the most powerful nation on earth. Your currency is strong because our commerce is flourishing. Our navy is the envy of the world. And yet you would turn your back on all this and leave us. Why? To rejoin a people of lowly status whose gods are not even visible!" Often, when I think of that exchange, I say to myself that the high priest's logic was pretty convincing.

François Mitterrand: Moses was a great man, not just a simple prince, precisely because he failed to heed that logic.

Elie Wiesel: According to Jewish tradition, Moses was the name given him by Princess Batya, the daughter of the Pharaoh. Actually, Moses had seven names, but the only one that stuck was the one given him by Batya. The Talmud explains that it was out of gratitude — a very deep-rooted Jewish virtue, anchored in our collective memory — that we retained that name. But while we're on the subject of the Bible, can we talk a little about Jacob wrestling with the Angel?

François Mitterrand: That is an episode I find difficult to explain symbolically.

Elie Wiesel: The Angel was the supreme enemy.

François Mitterrand: If I recall my readings on the subject correctly, angels are a fairly recent invention, dating from about a century before Christ. The Christian church picked up the notion and integrated it into its own thinking and dogma, and later on a number of Christian heresies subsumed them into their own sects with even greater imaginative power. What I find bizarre is that that legend should bring the Angel into Jacob's story, when Jacob lived long before the concept even existed.

Elie Wiesel: The term does appear in the Bible.

François Mitterrand: The Bible is a very complicated mixture of fact and legend. It's extremely difficult, if you're not a biblical scholar, to distinguish between the original text and the later extrapolations. Did the Angel first appear a century before Christ, or did it make its appearance much earlier? That's something I can't say with any degree of assurance.

Elie Wiesel: The Angel was there; the interpretation came later. The biblical term is *malakh,* which means "messenger." When Jacob was wrestling with the Angel, it was the messenger of God he was fighting with.

François Mitterrand: And do we know why?

Elie Wiesel: Perhaps in order to become Israel. In any case, these are among the most obscure pages of the Bible. But today, Israel is a political phenomenon that fills me with anguish. Everywhere one looks, the situation looks hopeless.

François Mitterrand: It's up to the leaders of the various countries involved to work their way through the morass of difficulties and find the best solution. On the one hand, in the most ancient Jewish lands Jews are currently in the minority; and on the other, certain Jewish leaders seem tempted to seize territories that have no relation to Jewish history. The situation is both complicated and confusing. There is to my mind a solution to the problem, but I'll refrain from voicing it, since I would be taxed with being pretentious. I do however think it imperative for both sides to shed themselves of the notion of domination. To be sure, one must stand firm on the matter of the right to live on this land; but those involved must also learn to be more malleable, humbler, careful not to let their love of country become an instinct for domination. The problem is, not only the political leaders but the people themselves tend to confuse the will to survive with the will to dominate. In the relation between Jews and Arabs, both within Israel itself and the territories of Trans Jordan, the problem has to be faced day in and day out. I think that in the case of Trans Jordan, the Palestinians have the right to a national entity; yet they cannot deny the Israeli people, the Jewish people, its legitimate historical rights.

Elie Wiesel: Mr. President, the world is well aware of our friendship. In the wake of the revelations about your political past that appeared for the most part in the autumn of 1994, all sorts of people have besieged me with questions about your relations with René Bousquet. I must add that these revelations have not only raised doubts in people's minds, they have been a cause of serious concern.

René Bousquet was general secretary of the Vichy police, and as such was a key contact between Vichy and the German occupation police, especially the hated Knochen and Oberg. He was at worst the instigator and at best the organizer of the anti-Jewish roundups, the power behind a French police force that was, during those dark days, largely corrupt; the man who helped fill the human quotas for the Nazi death camps. All that upsets me all the more because I am well aware of your past in the French Resistance movement, your courage as a member of the underground, your contribution to the survival of the state of Israel, and your affection for the Jewish people.

All this said, these people would never forgive me or understand if I failed to ask you, clearly and unequivocally, these questions. For those who love you as well as those who are trying to understand exactly what happened back then, I would like to hear, directly from you, what you have to say about all this, candidly and completely.

Were you in fact in contact with René Bousquet during the war, after your arrival in Vichy? If so, what precisely were the relations between you? Were they dictated by the demands of your work in the Resistance? And was that also the reason — I mean your role in the Resistance — you were in contact with a number of René Bousquet's close collaborators at the time, some of whom, a dozen or so years after the war, became politically involved with you, as members of your cabinet, as Minister of the Interior in one instance?

François Mitterrand: I'm going to respond to these questions and concerns because you are the one raising them. I must say I feel no obligation to respond to those who, whatever their motives, set themselves up as judge and jury. First, I did not know René Bousquet during the war. However, in 1942, 1943, and 1944 I was in contact with a certain Jean-Paul Martin, who was not, as you suggest, one of Bousquet's close collaborators but who did work with the head of the Vichy police, a man who reported to Bousquet. This was, as you well know, a time of extraordinary complexity and a period of great danger. You had to have forged documents that looked more official than the real ones; you had to have your papers properly stamped at all times to avoid being arrested by the constant controls; you had to have tried and true friends who could help extricate you from tricky situations. Those friends did indeed help me in my Resistance efforts, as they helped many others in various ways.

You must remember that Vichy was not one monolithic bloc, nor was the Resistance for that matter. There were times and places where the two came together in a common cause. The struggle against the occupying forces took on many and varied forms. Jean-Paul Martin, for example, informed us several times of impending roundups, of house searches that would be taking place in a few hours or a few days. He saved a lot of lives, and I'm forever grateful to him for what he did.

Was René Bousquet aware of what his lieutenant was doing? I have no way of knowing. In any case, I never met him in those days.

Elie Wiesel: If, as you've just confirmed to me and as you've already told a number of historians who were researching this period, you met René Bousquet for the first time in 1949, were you unaware of his wartime past? Given the major political posts you filled during the 1950s, you certainly had the investigative means at your disposal to obtain this information.

François Mitterrand: I knew that René Bousquet had been a member of the Vichy government. I knew that he had been a prefect during the Third Republic. And I knew that after he resigned his Vichy post, he had been deported by the Germans. That was as much as I knew, no matter what so-called investigative sources might have been at my disposal.

Do you think for a minute that any minister, even a minister of the Interior ten years after the event, calls for the complete police file on each of his visitors? That's simply not the way things are done. That may be the way people imagine it's done. What is more, don't be so naive as to think that there aren't times when the appropriate authorities are not tempted, in certain cases, to "cleanse" the files in question.

In the 1950s, René Bousquet was a man who had been fully exonerated by the High Court of Justice. I remind you that that same court, which in many instances had imposed death sentences on a great number of collaborators, had sentenced Bousquet to "five years of national indignity," which was little more than a slap on the wrist, then immediately revoked that sentence because of his Resistance record. I did not feel it was my role to second-guess either the High Court or the prosecutors. I should add, too, that for the following three decades — that is, until 1978 — when a certain Darquier de Pellepoix — a man of dubious reputation to say the least — publicly accused Bousquet of having participated in the roundup of Jews at the Vél d'Hiv in Paris[9] — he frequented various political salons (to which I was not invited), was a member of several boards of directors, and was friends with all sorts of eminent personalities, all of whom conveniently seem to have forgotten they ever knew the man. All of which to say that René Bousquet, after the war, was surrounded by an aura of respectability. He held as I recall a high administrative post at the Bank of Indochina; he was a member of the board of the daily newspaper *La Dépêche de Midi*, a paper of impeccable reputation to which I contributed a number of editorials over the years.

---

[9] Vél d'Hiv is short for Vélodrome d'Hiver, an indoor sports arena and bicycle racetrack in Paris often used for political rallies. During the German occupation, it was also used as a staging area for Jews rounded up in raids.

Elie Wiesel: When you returned from captivity in Germany, you declared that you were unaware of the anti-Jewish laws, adding — and this especially hurt many of your friends, many of our friends — that as a matter of fact these laws only affected foreign Jews; that is, non-French Jews. Could you clarify that for us?

As time went on, after you returned to France, you could not help but be aware of that anti-Jewish legislation, if only by noting the people in the street who were obliged to wear the yellow Star of David. How did you feel when you saw that?

François Mitterrand: First, you have to understand that when we were in captivity in Germany, there was no way we could keep up with the new legislation emanating from Vichy in those days. Besides, we had other, more immediate concerns. As for myself, I was entirely focused on one overriding preoccupation, which was to escape at all costs. And when I did manage to escape and make my way back to France, I did not rush to read the latest issue of the official government bulletin. And, of course, I saw the yellow Stars of David, and learned of the laws that had been passed ordering all Jews to wear them. That law, and that knowledge, went a long way toward turning me away from a system that condoned such a crime. And I fought against it. I went to England, to Algeria, then returned to occupied France in February, 1944, where I was part of a select group appointed by de Gaulle to assume power as soon as Paris was liberated. The discovery, when the concentration camps were liberated in 1945, of the indescribable horror of the Nazi persecutions established my deep-rooted attachment both to the defense and the survival of Israel, my commitment to that cause since the early days of the Fourth Republic. You know my commitment not only to the question of Israel's survival but to peace in the Middle East. I've said all I'm going to say on the subject.

Elie Wiesel: There is another question, one that in my view is the most important. I can conceive that a politician has to slant things when he writes. And I can imagine that political acts have laws and constraints that differ from those of common morality. I can even understand — however much that knowledge pains me personally — that for several decades you carried on a relationship with René Bousquet because it seemed to you politically necessary or expedient, even if I find it morally reprehensible. I can accept the necessity; I refuse to accept the legitimacy.

In the course of the various interviews you granted in the fall of 1994, you seemed be trying to rehabilitate René Bousquet, make him appear as Mr. Nice Guy, a man who was not only competent but brilliant, exceptional both physically and mentally. The fact remains, this is the same man who handed over little Jewish children to the Nazis, who weren't even pressuring him to go to such lengths!

I can conceive that politics sometimes involves siding with Evil, but only because one intends to use Evil for some noble purpose; and I can understand that in the course of fulfilling one's political functions one has upon occasion to press into service people whose reputations are less than impeccable, people one would doubtless not be seen with under other circumstances. But from that general notion to ignoring the past of a man like René Bousquet, glossing over his collusion with the Vichy government, not to mention the photos of him hobnobbing with several high officers of the Gestapo! René Bousquet failed both humanity and honor. Why try to endow him with human qualities that he simply did not have?

François Mitterrand: I don't greatly appreciate your remarks about politicians' slanting things, as if politics and morality were mutually exclusive. Furthermore, your phillipic conveniently ignores the chronology of events. In 1949, Bousquet was, I repeat, completely exonerated by the French judicial system, which in those days was particularly severe. He went on to fulfill a number of public and governmental posts of which we're all aware. At that point I was a government minister in the Fourth Republic myself. And like everyone else, I met René Bousquet in the exercise of my various functions. But only rarely. In 1978 he was implicated in the terrible Vél d'Hiver scandal by a man who, as I said, was a man of dubious reputation, Darquier de Pellepoix, who had fled France and sought refuge in Franco's Spain. A man of such impeccable reputation as Serge Klarsfeld, one of the world's most respected Nazi hunters, did not lodge a complaint against Bousquet until 1989. The knowledge of the same facts on which Klarsfeld based his complaint led me to stop seeing Bousquet in 1986. I simply said to several interviewers, when they raised the question recently, the same thing I told you today, namely what I thought of him as a man. He was in fact direct, intelligent, even brilliant. He was physically courageous. As a young subprefect during the 1930s, when the southwest of France was inundated with deadly floods, he personally rescued several people, who without him would surely have drowned, and was awarded the Legion of Honor by President Lebrun. People who worked with him through the years always stressed that he was loyal. Why do you want me to tell you otherwise? I'm not a man who changes his opinion about his colleagues just because the world has come down on them.

You say that he is Evil incarnate. But Evil is rarely incarnate in a single man, any more in fact than is Good. Monsters are as rare in this world as saints.

That Bousquet committed errors, I do not deny. That these errors led to crimes is unfortunately also true. That these crimes deserved to be investigated, to determine to what degree he was the moving force behind them, or an accomplice, was for the courts to decide. That René Bousquet's errors led him beyond the pale of the justifiable, recent historical discoveries have established beyond a shadow of doubt. Perhaps he put too much store in his intelligence, which I continue to maintain was exceptional; perhaps he thought he could salvage as much as he could by his actions, however horrible that complicity might appear to us today. The fact is, he deceived himself, he did go astray. And I categorically deny that I'm trying to rehabilitate him, as you suggest. I'm simply telling you what happened as I see it.

I do agree with you that memory is a duty. I did all I could to make sure the memory of anti-Semitic persecutions would not be forgotten and to do justice to those who were its victims. But you must also understand this. France is a country of disconcerting diversity. My role, as president of the Republic, was to bring people together, to keep united the various elements in a country where, without that constant effort, they would tend to drift apart. My mission was to express and ensure the country's unity, to guarantee its indivisibility.

I have never felt complacent about any of these various areas, but I had to be careful not to allow any elements to go astray and light the fires of disunion, which are only too ready to reignite. Over the past century France has been subjected to all manner of civil wars, both latent and declared: between the republicans and the monarchists, between the Dreyfusards and the anti-Dreyfusards,[10] between Church and State. Then there were the burning social issues before the war that split the country; the war itself and the German occupation, followed by the decolonization after the war — all of which were subjects of intense passion among the French, and, I would say, so many subjects of division among them. My role was to keep divisive elements under control. And indeed I did not wish or desire to reopen judicial decisions that had already been settled by the relevant authorities.

Elie Wiesel: My own feeling is that how you look back at your past is as important as your past itself. When last we met you admitted that you thought you may have made some mistakes during this period, that you perhaps were not as vigilant as you should have been. Is that an expression of regret, or even remorse?

François Mitterrand: Referring specifically to the case you

---

[10] The case of Captain Alfred Dreyfus (1859–1935), an Alsatian Jew accused of espionage in 1894, divided France and caused anti-Semitic violence. Among the Dreyfusards were Emile Zola and Marcel Proust. Among the anti-Dreyfusards was Maurice Barrès.

brought up, namely that of René Bousquet, I feel neither regret nor remorse. None whatsoever. And do you want to know why? Because this "trial" to which I have been subjected on the matter makes my blood boil. I am trying to look back at my life in all objectivity, to see it from the perspective of the man I am today, having accomplished what I've accomplished, knowing what I know, from today's viewpoint. In other words, near the end of my life.

First of all, I shall say that over the course of the years I have shed the restrictions and restraints of my background, my education, and my early prejudices. I much prefer having followed the path I did, moving increasingly away from the conservative environment out of which I came toward the ideals of the Left, rather than taking the opposite road, which many of my contemporaries followed, especially during the years just before and during World War II. This path was not without its bumps and setbacks, but I *did* make it, and I must confess to feeling a certain pride when I look back and see how far I have come.

Also, to comment on your remark that political action has its restrictions; indeed, it has its laws. That may be true, but it never forces you to do something contrary to what you believe. One of Malraux's heroes in *Man's Hope* says, "Action thinks of itself only in terms of action," which is partly true. But today, with the benefit of hindsight, and knowing what I know, I try to judge what I've done as objectively as possible. And I can honestly say that I am at peace with myself.

III

WAR

Elie Wiesel: Wars have images. Mine is of a father leaving home. He's holding his suitcase and he's saying good-bye to his children, who have accompanied him down to the train station. My image of war is always someone leaving. What are your images?

François Mitterrand: I would be hard pressed to give you images that were universal. Perhaps had you asked me that question before 1939, or if I had not been swept up in a war myself, I might respond differently. My images are linked to what I lived through in France in 1939: enormous numbers of poorly trained soldiers being sent off to fight without knowing why. These men are not necessarily unhappy about being shipped off, because the tedium of their lives has been broken, but they are ignorant of war's terrors. From the point of view of a country defeated from the outset, war is catastrophe, a gigantic migratory upheaval. All social structures suddenly collapse and take with them any fixed sense of place, so masses of people go around in circles with no idea where they should go. It's as if someone had kicked an ant hill. War means disorientation for hundreds of thousands of people because the certainties that had guided their lives are gone.

Those are the images I see, because they are what I saw.

Elie Wiesel: Where were you when war was declared?

François Mitterrand: I was walking down Boulevard Saint-Michel with Georges Dayan. We were listening to the news and to Daladier's[11] appeals to action. I was twenty-three and fresh out of law school. Dayan and I were doing our military service, but we were walking along Boulevard Saint-Michel like two civilians. Our barracks were located on Boulevard Port-Royal and we could come and go freely. We had the clear sense, that day, that from then on nothing would be the same as before. The paths of our lives had split. "Look at Boulevard Saint-Michel," we were saying. "Look at the students around us and at the shops — none of this will be the same. When we come home from the war we will not be what we are now." It was such a poignant feeling. We knew that war meant the end of our youth, possibly the end of our lives, and certainly the end of the world we had known. That was our first reaction. It was self-centered because we interpreted what was happening in terms of ourselves. After that, everything seemed to fall apart. I found myself caught up in crowds. All those individual human destinies jostling against one another.

Elie Wiesel: How did people react? Were they stunned? In shock?

François Mitterrand: The older generation, which had gone through World War I, looked on in terrible silence. They

[11] Edouard Daladier (1884–1970) was prime minister of France just before World War II. It was his government that joined the British declaration of war against the Germans on September 3, 1939.

knew that in a modern world war the first wave of soldiers had little chance of coming back. But no one said anything.

So for me the first images were classic ones — being transported to the front in horse-drawn wagons, in which for hours at a time we sat with our legs dangling over the side, watching the countryside roll by, going we-knew-not-where, innocent of what lay ahead.

From then on, you don't live day-by-day; you live minute-by-minute. You live from one minute to the next and that is all you do.

Elie Wiesel: There is comfort in that. Someone else is in charge of your life and you have no decisions to make.

François Mitterrand: For some, the change was an adventure. A reprieve from their stifled lives.

Elie Wiesel: War means there must be an enemy. Did you think of Germany as the enemy?

François Mitterrand: No, something else. We had no desire to cross swords with the Germans, nor to kill them. We were sophisticated enough not to confuse Nazism with the Germans. Nazism was an ideology, an evil force that had taken hold of the German people and taken them in.

Elie Wiesel: You were twenty-three years old. What were your political leanings?

François Mitterrand: I had none. I was curious about everything, literature as much as politics. I went to a number of political rallies and gatherings run by the anti-Fascist committees, and to those organized by the intellectuals of the day, like

André Gide, André Malraux, Julien Benda, and others; I went to small meetings, such as the ones organized by the Union for the Truth; I listened to Georges Bernanos and François Mauriac.[12] I also walked a great deal. I must have spent more time walking than I did studying. In short, I was interested in politics but had not committed myself politically. The small forays I had made immediately left me feeling bored and unimpressed.

Elie Wiesel: So you knew a little about what was happening in Germany?

François Mitterrand: Yes, but we had only a vague idea about the concentration camps. We knew of course that German dissidents were being interned. It would be some time yet before we knew the shocking truth about the camps.

Elie Wiesel: Kristallnacht had already taken place. At the beginning of November 1938 a young German Jew assassinated a German diplomat. As punishment, hundreds of synagogues were set on fire, Jewish stores looted, men humiliated, beaten, locked up.[13]

---

[12] André Gide (1869–1951) is best known for his novel *The Counterfeiters* (1925). André Malraux (1901–1976) was a writer, philosopher, politician, art historian, and the author of *Man's Fate* (1933) and *Man's Hope* (1937). Julien Benda (1867–1956) wrote *The Betrayal of the Intellectuals*, which militated against preoccupation with earthly values and the disappearance of spiritual ones. Georges Bernanos (1888–1948), a Catholic writer and intellectual, subscribed to a medieval view of chivalry.

[13] Kristallnacht ("night of broken glass") refers to the vicious pogrom that took place following the assassination of Ernst von Rath.

François Mitterrand: Everyone knew about the assassination of von Rath. We also knew that Jews were being persecuted. But we had no clear sense what Kristallnacht meant.

Elie Wiesel: The press must have talked about it. Yet you weren't aware of it?

François Mitterrand: No.

Elie Wiesel: I find it fascinating that in 1939 a man such as you, keen as you were about justice and therefore about the notion of justice, didn't yet know that Nazism . . .

François Mitterrand: There were certainly people who knew. But the information we were getting was contradictory. We had become aware of Jewish persecution, which had already started. The von Rath affair, if it had repercussions, didn't provide us with a way of grasping what they were. We were already at war.

Elie Wiesel: When war broke out in 1939, it wasn't real, correct? Neither the enemy nor the image were real.

François Mitterrand: Absolutely correct. All we had was an idea. There had been those huge rallies at Nuremberg, the mobilization and the militarization of Germany, and plenty of other disquieting events. Basically, though, we had a long way to go yet before we fully understood what had happened in Germany.

Elie Wiesel: Yet in 1938 you wrote an article about Munich.

François Mitterrand: The article I wrote was about the *Anschluss* and therefore looked further back than the Munich

Agreement. Of course I was already making political choices, as you're suggesting, but I didn't consider myself committed to any particular course of action. Writing is action, I admit. What I mean is that I was a member of no organized group. My reactions were personal. My best friend, Georges Dayan, whom as I mentioned earlier I saw all the time — every day — was Jewish. He had grown up in a Jewish environment in which people stayed among themselves, as if they had all come to Paris together from the provinces. I was not part of that milieu, but all my best friends at the time were, so I was very sensitive to their problems.

Elie Wiesel: Did you think France would win the war?

François Mitterrand: There was so much chaos and the Republic was so weak that I couldn't think that. I wrote the article on the *Anschluss* you just alluded to in April 1938, when I was twenty-one, and called it "This Far and No Farther." The title came from a phrase Austrian Chancellor Schuschnigg had used after he'd agreed to negotiate with Hitler. What my article emphasized was that when someone says "this far," things always go farther. When Chancellor Schuschnigg told Hitler, "This far and no farther," German troops had already received the order to move into Austria. Here is what I wrote:

> Because power has already broken through it could never have been prevented from doing so in the first place. Who dares to suggest that the powerful would be willing to set limits on themselves? Those who are powerless, that's who — those who derive courage from talking, from believing that they have fixed a boundary to power and a rationale to their own concessions.

"This far and no farther." Why would the powerful go "this far" without intending to go farther? We tend to ignore the historical and scientific truth that if something has worked once, it will be tried again.

In the lives of nations as much as in the lives of individuals, retreat means surrender. A strategic withdrawal but masks defeat; and any attempt to mitigate or justify retreat, or to refuse responsibility for it, alters not the fact that man condemns himself from the moment of his first fall. What is purity if it is sullied? What is will if it bends? What is liberty if it yields? Later there may come an opportunity for recoup and revenge, but by then blood and sacrifice are mercenary.

When Cardinal Innitzer adds "Heil Hitler" to his letter, all he does is spare his country for a few more days. There is nothing to fear so long as he is needed. He too declares that he can accept things "this far," but no farther. Will anyone care what he thinks when things go farther?

France, England, and Italy take note of the *Anschluss,* but more or less dryly indicate their acceptance. "Okay! That's it! No more blackmail! Our armies are stirred up! Our peoples are fed up! Do you hear us? This far and no farther!" This is what they call peevishness. Peevishness, however, has never been a substitute for rage.

Moderation is a virtue when based on justice; it is convenient to confuse justice with popular will. Hence the justification for a plebiscite. Popular will says Austria is really another Germany, a Germany of waltzes, wit, the Danube, Vienna, Mozart—just like those images in all those classic prints. When we broke up the Austro-Hungarian Empire the Empire lost its soul. It is meet that a lighthearted and ambitious Austria should enjoy the favors of an emperor and receive the garland of an archduchess; around it are the grumbling Slav and warlike

Czech. Once, there was a parliament, and it provided a fine occasion for everyone to express his wishes. It also supplied a handy excuse for doing nothing. Those who talk have no love for action. Anyway, all that is gone and forgotten. The shadow of the neighbor, a trifle too somber perhaps but very mysterious (and mystery has its appeal), began to spread. Money, finances, markets, the power and the right to flaunt power and unity. What prodigious lovers these make! Yes, Prussia with its heavy-handed squires is watchful, but Vienna is alive and once again rules at the heart of Europe: once again the world will come and bow before her when she shows she has the power to back up her charm. If the Teuton dances with two left feet and treads on the toes of his waltz partner, he is still to be celebrated because he is triumphant. And when a man is triumphant he has the right to be ugly.

Thus is a greater Germany born of defeat. What Austria was not able to achieve at the height of its glory, what Prussia wouldn't or couldn't manage during its days of hegemony, has been achieved by losing a war. Old Schwartzenberg and that moderate Bismarck — who had refused to leave Austria after Sadova in 1866 — have met their master. For its part, the German Reich has re-found its loyal two-headed eagle, one head looking East, the other West. Austria is no longer but a German province. American President Woodrow Wilson's work has been undone. The masses that yesterday thronged Vienna's avenues to cheer Schuschnigg today heap praise on their new master. Tanks and cannons rumble through the streets. Doctors and professors explain that what was inevitable has been given its due. Perhaps that is so. Might makes right and can assume the veneer of justice. Austria is German! Austrian culture is German culture! Austria is the necessary complement to a Germanic empire.

Perhaps it is true that it would be folly for France to wage a war to save a peace that has already been lost. Perhaps it is true that the death of a single man is a graver matter than the destruction of a nation. Everything points me to the conclusion that nothing justifies a revolt against what is. Yet still I feel a certain disquiet. Among the enthusiastic crowds in Innsbruck and Vienna I perceive the anguish of one lonely face, leaning over the blue Danube, and I try in vain not to see it reflect the torrent of the river. In the wake of the triumphant arrival of the god of Bayreuth in the land of Mozart, I sense what sacrilege is brewing, and despite myself I feel a kind of shame, as if I knew I were responsible.

Elie Wiesel: You had already found your voice. Where did you publish that?

François Mitterrand: In a small student magazine. The *Anschluss,* the "triumphant arrival of the god of Bayreuth in the land of Mozart," foreshadowed the sacrilege in the works. It was a premonition of Hitler's triumph over Europe.

Elie Wiesel: I had asked you if you had thought France could win the war. You said no.

François Mitterrand: One always hopes. At the time, however, I didn't have a sufficiently clear view of matters. The condition of the government, the institutions, public opinion, the disarray of the armies, and the absence of organization and materiel — all these left me feeling very pessimistic.

Elie Wiesel: How terrifying it is to be a soldier in an army on the verge of defeat, a citizen of a country about to be vanquished — though today we know that France's military power was superior to Germany's.

François Mitterrand: So they say. France may have had a large enough air force, but it lacked sufficient armored divisions.

Elie Wiesel: What seemed to be lacking was strategy.

François Mitterrand: I clung to the rather naive belief, as irrational as all beliefs are, that we would eventually win the war — as turned out to be the case. But I was a soldier in that first wave, that one that was crushed by the onslaught in May–June 1940.

Elie Wiesel: Where were you during the Phony War[14]?

François Mitterrand: At the front lines, meaning on that part of French soil located to the east of the Maginot Line. The line was designed to act as a safety valve in the event of a German offensive. It was necessary to have troops deployed ahead of it to warn of an attack. The Maginot Line didn't run right along the border — there was still a little French soil on the eastern side of it. That's where I found myself, in a regiment of the colonial infantry. There were few skirmishes, though we did sometimes come under fire and from time to time we were shelled. The front lines were manned by small segments of the

---

[14] The so-called Phony War marks the period between France and England's declaration of war on Germany in September of 1939, and the actual outbreak of war in June of 1941. France's principal line of defense against a German attack was the Maginot Line, a series of fortifications constructed along the French-German border.

army. We could see that the Germans had taken up positions behind barbed wire five hundred meters away. Yet it was still a phony war for us. For those farther from the front it was even more of one. People began to forget all about the war.

A little before May I was sent to the northern end of the Maginot Line in the Ardennes, near Montmédy, where there were no fortifications. It was a kind of void, located between the Maginot Line and Sedan, twenty miles to the east. They kept us busy digging gardens and trenches. We started to forget about the war. Then in the early hours of May 10, 1940 came a continuous rumble. German planes were passing overhead. The noise they made was ominous and impressive. From then on it was war. The Germans came at us with tanks. On the morning of May 10, we watched them take up positions on the edge of a small stream called the Chiers, the border with Belgium, and they began their offensive from there. The real war began. For me it lasted until June 14, the day I was wounded. During that month I knew real combat, direct, face-to-face contact with an enemy.

Elie Wiesel: What were you doing? How did you spend your days?

François Mitterrand: First I was in command of an infantry unit. We dug foxholes and set up machine-gun posts to stop the German advance, but we couldn't. The order came to fall back, so we started to retreat in stages along the Meuse. This was an exhausting process because we had to keep moving and still try to slow the Germans down. We alternated with a regiment from the Foreign Legion, but there was no time for sleep.

Elie Wiesel: Did you suffer heavy losses?

François Mitterrand: Yes, right from the start. In my company there was only one senior officer left and I was one of the last junior officers.

Elie Wiesel: Did you lose men close to you? Friends?

François Mitterrand: In my section, yes, several. I got along well with quite a few of the men. One was a corporal from Lannion named Bodium. He was a terrific guy. He was ripped apart by a shell. There was nothing left of him. I remember one guy from Vendé named Trotin, also very nice — kind, reliable, courageous. He was killed as well. And a fairly sophisticated fellow who ran nightclubs in Paris and had become convinced that he was going to die. He was in fact one of the first to be killed.

Elie Wiesel: How did seeing these first deaths affect you?

François Mitterrand: We were in combat. The shelling that was preparing the way for the German infantry attacks was deafening and awesome. All we thought about was surviving. Death was for others. Hope is a powerful life-force for the young.

Elie Wiesel: Today, experts say almost unanimously that had France attacked in 1939 it would have won the war.

François Mitterrand: There were huge debates about that at the time. Should or should we not launch a preemptive strike? Some, like Paul Reynaud, were in favor of it, but the majority was against the idea. This meant that from a strategic point of view we were constantly on the defensive. There was no movement in favor of aggression. We were ordered to defend and to resist as long as possible and that was it. Not good military strategy.

Elie Wiesel: So you think that this defensive war was a mistake?

François Mitterrand: I was never asked to advance, only to retreat. I cannot judge the logic of it, not knowing what state the armed forces were in at the time.

Elie Wiesel: One lesson that might be drawn is that sometimes a preventive war is justified.

François Mitterrand: If you are certain there is no way of avoiding war, then I believe you have the moral authority to use whatever means necessary to win it. Especially when it is a question of defending both your country and a vision of humanity. It would be hypocritical to say that whoever starts a war is wrong. Starting a war doesn't necessarily mean firing the first shot.

Elie Wiesel: What if someone had killed Hitler in 1936?

François Mitterrand: Political crimes are not justifiable. Yet — of course — that thought will always haunt us.

Elie Wiesel: I'm thinking of the British ambassador to Germany, who with great remorse said that he'd had a revolver in his pocket and could have killed Hitler. He regretted not having done it.

François Mitterrand: No one can ever know what repercussions political crimes will have. They turn us into judges. Were every individual to make himself into a judge, it would justify taking matters into one's own hands.

Elie Wiesel: Isn't that exactly what war does? Turn everyone into a judge, a victim, an executioner? War has an equalizing power.

François Mitterrand: There eventually were a few attempts on Hitler's life. They weren't numerous to begin with — fewer attempts than there were on the lives of Louis-Philippe and Napoléon III.

Elie Wiesel: If there were so few attempts on Hitler's life, it was because in the beginning he brought the Germans glory. He had taken back territory that belonged to Germany and thanks to him the country had become a power to be feared.

François Mitterrand: We must remember why Hitler was so successful for several years. It is a subject I often ponder. Rather than talk about domestic politics and racism we need, I think, to talk about Germany itself. So long as Hitler sought to overcome the effects of the Treaty of Versailles, to undo the 1918 defeat, and so long as he sought to unite the Germans under one state, success came easily. Even though he started in 1933, soon after the Treaty, Hitler knew that the Western powers, England and France in particular, had neither the capacity nor the will to stop someone whose actions the German people themselves thought, deep down, were justified. Hitler had one powerful idea: to unify the Germans. He pulled off the *Anschluss* — and the other countries were insufficiently prepared, ideologically and militarily, to oppose German unity. They gave in to him time after time. Hitler began to fail the moment he abandoned his own strategy, when he attacked Bohemia and took territory that was not German. From that moment on he started to lose ground. First Bohemia, then Poland. As soon as he turned himself into the conqueror of lands other than German, war was inevitable. He won the first round, lost the second.

Elie Wiesel: He was looking for war. Not just victory but, above all, war.

François Mitterrand: What I mean is that Hitler had been stunningly successful. He folded some eleven or twelve million people back into Germany without creating a serious crisis. That crisis — the war, in other words — started the moment he ceased acting simply as a nationalist patriot, a German expansionist, and set out to vanquish the world in the name of a savage ideology. I'm trying to locate that moment in history when, despite his formidable military triumphs, he had already lost.

Elie Wiesel: Do you think he would have remained in power longer had he not crossed that boundary? I think that if he had held power in 1939 without attacking France . . .

François Mitterrand: He didn't go after France, but after Bohemia and Czechoslovakia. France had treaties and the protection of alliances . . .

Elie Wiesel: Yes, though France would not have attacked.

François Mitterrand: As soon as he had resolved the German problem, or let us say the Germanic problem, he entered into a network of treaties, accords, and alliances despite the fact that he wanted war. Like others judging from hindsight, I believe that attempting to conquer Europe was doomed from the outset to be a death march. Had Hitler been content with simply reuniting the German peoples I doubt anyone would have challenged him.

Elie Wiesel: Let me push it further. In 1939, Germany occupied Poland. France and Great Britain declared war. Until May of 1940, however, nothing happened. There was no German offensive. Do you think that France and England would have eventually attacked Germany? I think not.

François Mitterrand: They had accepted Czechoslovakia's fate, which was already a source of shame for them, a diminution of their power, prestige, and authority. They couldn't accept having all their alliances torn to shreds.

Elie Wiesel: Nonetheless, they abandoned Poland.

François Mitterrand: They lacked resolve.

Elie Wiesel: And then the Soviet Union, which had made a pact with Hitler . . .

François Mitterrand: If you dig a little deeper you discover that the Russians feared Hitler but were also not happy with the Western nations. I think that from the Russian point of view we had made a number of diplomatic blunders.

Elie Wiesel: In the meantime you were getting beaten. You were retreating.

François Mitterrand: Yes, I was watching France fall apart and it was breaking my heart. I had no real way of knowing what was going on. I was too much in the thick of it.

Elie Wiesel: Did you feel humiliated?

François Mitterrand: I was filled with all sorts of rage.

Elie Wiesel: Rage about what?

François Mitterrand: The manner in which France had been led.

Elie Wiesel: Did you sense France would be defeated?

François Mitterrand: I have said I did. I knew very well how disorganized the army was. I played a part in that war and I knew that we had neither the heart or the materiel necessary to win it.

Elie Wiesel: Were you thinking about the future?

François Mitterrand: No. Perhaps I had the vague sense that despite everything we would get through. The campaign of 1940 was one of France's blackest moments.

Elie Wiesel: You felt this in your bones?

François Mitterrand: It has left an indelible mark on my life, and every time I have had occasion to protect France's sense of itself as a nation I think about that time. Never again will the country find itself in that situation.

Elie Wiesel: Did you come into contact with civilians during your retreat?

François Mitterrand: With the refugees crowding the roads in what was a general panic — yes. What was most terrible was that wherever we went we found no one. The villages were deserted, the houses abandoned. The French themselves had plundered them. The Germans couldn't have done it because they weren't even there yet. We would stop in a village to rest or sleep and I would go into a house to find the quilts slashed, the curtains ripped down, mirrors and glasses smashed, preserves splattering the floors, making them look like a painter's palette. All for nothing. Purely for the sake of destruction. The instinct of the horde.

Elie Wiesel: How do you explain it?

François Mitterrand: It was war. From the first second, civilization had evaporated and lawlessness took over. We were in a part of Lorraine that was French politically and German culturally. I was the first soldier to arrive and everything had already been looted. It was like entering Pharaoh's tomb, only to discover that it has been pillaged. Someone was there before you. War lays waste to every social structure and unleashes a whole range of primal urges. And a soldier, even one who has been defeated and doesn't yet know it, feels like an invader, even within his own country.

Elie Wiesel: A sad commentary. One would have hoped for greater solidarity.

François Mitterrand: Not then. Nothing held. All sorts of collective moral values had disappeared. France's failure in 1940 was brought about by a collapse of the spirit. This did not happen by accident. France had strengths, means, riches, and if it failed to marshal them it was because its very spirit had been crushed.

Elie Wiesel: Might one say that France had been defeated before it was defeated?

François Mitterrand: It must be said. The ruling classes had tried to seek revenge for their own political and social defeat by blaming the Popular Front.[15] We called it all a disaster and it truly was. I saw it from the inside. When I was wounded on June 14, they put me on a stretcher and a fellow soldier pushed me along the road to take me someplace I could get medical attention. Enemy planes were strafing the road. I saw an enormous procession of wagons, every one piled high with everything people could take from the houses — sheets, mattresses, armoires, chairs — in an overflowing heap, and pulled by a donkey or a horse, or cattle. It was one colossal traffic jam for miles on end, a dark line heading south and stretching all the way to the horizon. German planes added to the general panic by swooping down and firing their machine-guns. The soldier pushing me was a brave man but he did what everyone else did. He jumped into a ditch or made for the trees. I lay right in the middle of the road on my stretcher. I remember how alone I felt stretched out beneath the sky, watching the planes open fire.

Elie Wiesel: Where had you been wounded?

---

[15] Popular Front for Defense against Fascism was the full name of the Socialist party headed by Léon Blum that came to power in 1936.

François Mitterrand: A shell had exploded above a small unit I was forming with my junior officer, a young man my age — a professor of philosophy in the United States, where he had been connected with the French cultural attaché in Washington — with whom I was close. I was struck by two pieces of shrapnel. One hit just below the shoulder blade. I didn't even know it right away. I thought I'd been hit head on by a bullet. There was numbness around my throat. I told my friend, who'd been hit in the knee, that I'd been shot in the throat. This was ridiculous, because had that been the case I wouldn't have been able to speak. He ripped open my shirt — which meant that for two months I didn't have a shirt — and said, "There's nothing there, you haven't been hit." Then on closer inspection he saw a trickle of blood running down my back from a small hole. A fragment had lodged itself in my shoulder. There was another wound, but it was superficial. For a full year afterward my arm was a little stiff. I was as much in shock as wounded and was carried to a small road, which is where I found that stretcher. I was pushed several miles to the town of Esne-en-Argonne, where a nursing station had been set up in a cellar. Dozens of people were waiting for treatment, all far more seriously wounded than I, and surgeons worked at tables and amid groans. I left. I went to five hospitals without finding a doctor. By this point I was getting used to my wound. After all, I wasn't dead! I had never been treated by a doctor. When the Germans entered Paris I was still in Verdun. None of us knew that we were already prisoners of war, because the German army had cut Lorraine off, and so we kept going around in circles. Then came the Armistice. I was in the little town of Bruyère, in the Vosges, when the Germans arrived. I was lying in a hospital bed. In the bed next to mine was a Senegalese soldier.

Elie Wiesel: Were you taken prisoner?

François Mitterrand: No one bothered. They took over the town and the hospital, which henceforth fell under German authority. I didn't even notice the difference.

Elie Wiesel: What did it feel like to find yourself a prisoner?

François Mitterrand: It was life once again taking a new course. I was obsessed by one idea: escape. I immediately began making plans. Since I was not in very good shape physically — I was still weak and my arm was stiff — I was transported to the hospital at Lunéville, where the only care I got was tetanus shots. I came up with an escape plan. It wouldn't have been very hard to leave at that point. Then I was transferred to a camp for Lunéville prisoners. Nothing was the same behind barbed wire. Soon after that I was put on a convoy bound for Germany.

Elie Wiesel: How many of you were there?

François Mitterrand: Hundreds, all crammed together the same way others would later be deported in huge supply trains. We were taken to the heart of Germany. Again all I thought about was escaping. By this point it was August 1940. I escaped for the first time in March 1941, and was picked up three weeks later. In November I tried again, this time from a central camp. When I was recaptured I was transferred to a makeshift camp located on the old German border. I escaped from there twelve days later.

Elie Wiesel: Were the Germans singling Jews out from among the French?

François Mitterrand: No, but they were compiling files on everyone. I had a very good friend named Bernard, a Russian Jew. When they asked him, he told them that he was Jewish.

Elie Wiesel: Did he stay until the end?

François Mitterrand: He was with me the whole time. There was the appearance of legality. We were French soldiers in uniform and the Geneva Conventions were in force.

Elie Wiesel: What was life in the camps like?

François Mitterrand: Those Jews who spoke fluent German very quickly became important. They acted as our interpreters. They had declared their religion and the Germans called each of them "the Jew." For the most part our guards were German workers, men too old to be sent to the front, and good fellows.

Elie Wiesel: No SS?

François Mitterrand: They were at the front.

Elie Wiesel: The SS were at the front to kill Jews.

François Mitterrand: There were no SS actives in our camps.

Elie Wiesel: How did you spend your days?

François Mitterrand: The hours plodded by, punctuated by labor details. In the Kommandos you really worked. Schaala, which was near where I was in Rudolfstadt, consisted of 200 to 250 men, all housed in a fortified castle, a porcelain factory in Thuringe, in the old German Democratic Republic. I was part of a small unit of so-called intellectuals, because among our ranks were curates, schoolteachers, and some Spanish republicans. A curious mix, but we were all part of the French Army. We lived together and worked all day. Some jobs were exhausting, especially those involving digging. When the winter winds began to sweep across the plains of the region, conditions got rough. During the winter of 1941 I spent day after day shoveling snow from the tracks so that the trains could get through. It was tedious work. I wore what were called Russian socks — meaning rags — and naturally I was malnourished. I needed to summon my strength to survive.

Elie Wiesel: The most common image we have of those camps we owe to Sartre. He describes prisoners putting on plays and giving lectures.

François Mitterrand: This wasn't the case in the Kommandos. Our days were spent in hard labor and there wasn't time to think of anything else. In the evening we talked among ourselves. It was in the central camps, where there were twenty or thirty thousand men, that you found lecture programs.

Elie Wiesel: So you escaped in 1941.

François Mitterrand: I made my first attempt in March, my second in November, and finally succeeded in December 1941.

Elie Wiesel: You returned to France and France was occupied — but resisting.

François Mitterrand: I went straight down to the so-called Free Zone,[16] where the Vichy government was located.

Elie Wiesel: Did you get there on foot?

François Mitterrand: I took the train to Mouchard, located in the Jura mountains near the line of demarcation, which I crossed on foot at night. I found myself in the Free Zone but separated from my family, which had stayed behind in occupied France. Later I went to see my father in Charente several times by sneaking back across the border. Because I was an escapee, I led a secret life. And when the Germans entered the Free Zone I became an outlaw. So I lived like an outlaw — false papers, false everything.

Elie Wiesel: What name did you use?

François Mitterrand: I changed names several times. My best known *nom de guerre* was Morland. In England, the Free France Movement gave me the name Monnier. After the war I found at least forty phony identity cards. All of them came from Dieppe, which had been bombed and all records burned, so it was impossible to verify anything. At one point I called myself Basly, which was the name of someone who had actually ex-

---

[16] The southern half of France, not occupied by the Germans following their invasion of the country, was ostensibly governed by Maréchal Pétain's government in Vichy. The Germans invaded it in 1942, following the intentional scuttling of the French Navy in Marseilles by those who did not want the ships to fall into German hands.

isted. No doubt about it, I became very adept at forging false identity cards.

Elie Wiesel: There were tougher camps, places from which no one could escape.

François Mitterrand: Yes, the deportation camps.

Elie Wiesel: Those who escaped were wracked with guilt, because when someone succeeded in escaping others suffered for it.

François Mitterrand: That was true for us as well, except the punishment was light. Fellow prisoners had to remain standing all night. It was not torture, and it was not at all tragic. Discipline tightened. In the deportation camps, on the other hand, people were shot.

Elie Wiesel: Yet those who stayed behind urged others to escape. They wanted people to escape so that they could testify about what was happening.

François Mitterrand: I observed there were differences in the way prisoners were treated in the camps. When the newest arrivals were Russian and Serbian prisoners, conditions suddenly became horrific. That's when I realized how much better we were treated. The others went without any medical care and died of hunger. On the Serb side were wagons filled with corpses. We were given the job of throwing them into graves. The truth must be said: we French were better treated.

Elie Wiesel: So what did you know about my war, the war that came down upon us like a bolt of lightning? When did you know about it?

François Mitterrand: I'm not able to tell you. Before the war, we really were not aware of much. I knew about anti-Semitism through my mother, who had learned about it one day because of Paul Déroulède.[17] There were no Jews in Jarnac. At the turn of the century, my family was swept up by the patriotic fervor — my parents and grandparents being followers of Clemenceau and the Republicans — fueled by the humiliation of the 1870 defeat. Paul Déroulède was also a Chárontist. When he was exiled to San Sebastian, in Spain, my grandfather went to visit him on many occasions. It was a long trip. Once, he took my mother, who was seventeen and proud to meet Déroulède the "great patriot," the man who never accepted defeat. My mother was a good artist and brought him a painting of red, white, and blue flowers. Déroulède was pleased and they corresponded. I kept the letters Déroulède wrote to my mother. The day she visited him they were joined by the leaders of the anti-Dreyfusians and anti-Semite leagues. Everyone returned to France on the same train and in those days trains were slow. During the trip home the league members talked with my grandfather and my mother and the conversation turned to the Dreyfus affair and to anti-Semitic hate. My mother's eyes were gradually opened. When she got back to Jarnac she rebelled against anti-Semitism and never looked back. I still have her diary about the trip. In it she wrote, "This hate is not Christian." My parents were people of good will. At the end of the

[17] Paul Déroulède (1846–1914), writer and politician, founded the Patriots League (Ligue des patriotes) in 1882. The day after the funeral of President Félix Faure in 1899, he tried unsuccessfully to get the army to rise up against the parliamentary republic and was sentenced to ten years of exile.

Second World War, my father took in a young Jewish doctor named Stein and his wife. He became very fond of the man, who later committed suicide. My father was deeply pained by his death and he himself died not long afterward, saying "The world is crazy." The wife of the young doctor was remarried in the United States, to a Nobel Prize winner. She still comes to see us. During the war, those who were in danger of being deported talked about the anti-Semitism, but even they did not know the full extent of the nightmare. At the time it was more a question of fear than knowledge of a reality. Knowledge came after 1943, when eyewitness reports about the camps began arriving.

Elie Wiesel: Did the word *Auschwitz* mean anything to you in 1943?

François Mitterrand: It was an unknown word. We knew Dachau, I don't know how, and Buchenwald.

Elie Wiesel: Those were reeducation camps for political prisoners.

François Mitterrand: Our first Kommando was near Buchenwald.

Elie Wiesel: Were you aware of the torture, the medical experiments, the mass killings?

François Mitterrand: There were rumors, but they were far from real to us. At the end of the war, I was there when the Landsberg and Dachau concentration camps were liberated. General de Gaulle had sent me to accompany General Lewis. I saw bodies everywhere, many burned by flamethrowers. Then we understood. What you experienced is beyond language.

Elie Wiesel: Was your philosophy of humanity altered because of what you saw?

François Mitterrand: No, but hardened. In addition to the camps, testimony of what happened in the Warsaw Ghetto in 1943 was coming in from Jews who had been active participants, victims, and witnesses. A few survived to recount what they had seen.

Elie Wiesel: In addition to them were prisoners from Auschwitz who were trying to alert public opinion.

François Mitterrand: It took some time for them to be heard.

Elie Wiesel: The world already knew what was in their message. We know that in 1944, two months before the deportation of Hungarian Jews, two escaped prisoners from Auschwitz had given eyewitness testimony. They had seen that the ovens and gas chambers were being prepared for the six hundred thousand Hungarian Jews. They had told themselves that even if their chances of getting out were one in a million they had to warn the Hungarian Jews and the world. And they made it. They went to Hungary, to Czechoslovakia, they saw the apostolic nuncio, the leaders, and the resistance fighters. They were the first to describe what was happening. The whole world knew. Churchill and Roosevelt knew.

François Mitterrand: That was in March 1944. Near the end of the war.

Elie Wiesel: We were still in our homes in our little village, playing, studying, and, without knowing it, sentenced to death. Because two months later, in May, two weeks before Normandy, they started to deport Hungarian Jews.

François Mitterrand: Where were you at that time?

Elie Wiesel: In my little town in the Carpathians. The Germans occupied Hungary in March. In May, they began deporting one hundred thousand Jews each week. The death trains had priority over military convoys. The Wehrmacht was fighting on every front, but to Hitler the annihilation of the European Jews seemed more important than victory. When I think of the tragedy of Hungarian Jews, I am near despair, because people in Washington, in London, or in Stockholm were aware. They could have warned us and they didn't. Once we were in Auschwitz, we were lost. But we could have been saved. The Russians were ten miles from our ghetto. There were fifteen thousand of us, guarded by only two Germans and fifty-nine Hungarian gendarmes. We could have all quietly left the ghetto at night, every one of us.

François Mitterrand: I knew there were camps, but I was not aware of the systematic destruction. I did not imagine the reality of Auschwitz.

Elie Wiesel: Yet there were those reports from the Warsaw Ghetto.

François Mitterrand: Warsaw was not Auschwitz. The degree of suffering was unknown to me. You have heard testimony that never reached me.

Elie Wiesel: In my research I discovered that the major American newspapers, the *New York Times* and the *Washington Post,* were already talking about Auschwitz. People knew. Roosevelt knew but said nothing. One day I met President Carter. "I have a special gift for you," he said to me. "I asked the head of the CIA to look in the archives and find out everything we knew about the places where you were." They found photos taken by pilots after the bombardment of a factory near Auschwitz. They had studied them. Roosevelt had seen these same photos. It was so clear. I asked President Carter, "How is it possible that these photos were never used?" He replied, "I don't know." Then I asked him, "If you were me, what would you think about Roosevelt now?" The question seemed to trouble him. He looked closely at the photos and said nothing. I wondered if he would defend his predecessor, but he didn't. All he said later was, "Who knows what he could have thought?"

François Mitterrand: It had taken time for Roosevelt to get the United States into the war in the first place. He had had to convince public opinion.

Elie Wiesel: He was indifferent to what was happening to the Jews.

François Mitterrand: You believe that?

Elie Wiesel: He was afraid he would be accused of being too friendly with the Jews. I was not the first to suspect this and to write about it. Above all he did not want to be attacked by his enemies. Are there truths that a head of state must not say?

François Mitterrand: The timing of a difficult operation can require secrecy. Nothing else.

Elie Wiesel: If something tragic was happening and you were aware of it, would you speak out about it?

François Mitterrand: Yes. I did it for the Palestinians. The government had been silent about it for fear of confronting Syria, on which the fate of our hostages partly depended. And everyone was treating the Israeli government gently.

Elie Wiesel: Don't you think that war is nonetheless the worst of all outrages that can be inflicted upon the human spirit?

François Mitterrand: It is the worst collective outrage. Individual acts of violence are as serious. In and of itself war is not more cruel than the rape or the murder of a child.

Elie Wiesel: Why?

François Mitterrand: Because war is blind. What makes it so horrific is the scope of it, the huge numbers of people perishing together — an entire nation, a region, an ethnicity.

Elie Wiesel: The mutilation of a thousand children seems worse to me than the killing of one child. It was the same in Warsaw. But let us talk about nuclear war. What is it about nuclear war that gives you fear?

François Mitterrand: The annihilation of a part of humanity.

Elie Wiesel: Do you think it possible?

François Mitterrand: I am a proponent of France's nuclear arsenal because I believe that having these weapons makes any aggression against France impossible. As for a nuclear war between the superpowers, what has been created is a balance of terror. In the exercise of my duty to protect the fifty-five to sixty million compatriots for whom I was responsible, I followed what I believed to be the best strategy: possessing the means for dissuasion and response that would allow us to stand firm should the balance between East and West collapse.

Elie Wiesel: Have there already been imbalances?

François Mitterrand: None that lasted longer than three years.

Elie Wiesel: In your heart of hearts, do you think that the destruction of the planet possible?

François Mitterrand: Yes and no. Destructive as they are, nuclear arms are not enough to destroy the earth.

Elie Wiesel: I myself am especially afraid of an accident. Take the Challenger space shuttle, a vehicle everyone thought was as safe as possible. People believed they knew every cell and fiber. Yet the worst happened. Or take the Chernobyl nuclear power station. Russian experts no doubt maintained it with as much care as the Americans did the Challenger shuttle. Imagine Khaddafi with a nuclear bomb. I think of the children and their future, a future we are toying with.

François Mitterrand: We must count on every government's wisdom and every individual's fear. The question is, to what point does nuclear fear constitute the best defense?

Elie Wiesel: What can one do to prevent war?

François Mitterrand: Wage peace. Exercise infinite patience, the multiple resources of the human imagination and intelligence, and an ever firmer resolution. All this with one condition: knowing that, faced with a hostile country, we will sometimes need the resolve to wage war.

Elie Wiesel: Could you have imagined giving the order to press the button?

François Mitterrand: Political and military strategy are designed around preventing such an eventuality. Sometimes I did ask myself what I would have done were France in mortal danger. I would have exercised my freedom to act.

Elie Wiesel: A friend told me that you would have had seven minutes to decide whether to respond. The psychological pressure would be virtually unbearable.

François Mitterrand: Whoever decides must have the ability to wage war. As well as the ability to avoid war.

IV

WRITING AND LITERATURE

François Mitterrand: I believe we should be strictly professional and talk only about what we know. A more general, more universal grasp of things emerges by degrees. Some can attain the universal through philosophical, religious, or spiritual speculation. A few have been able to conceive of the whole range of knowledge, even though — I'm thinking here of Kant — their contact with the outside world was limited to strolling a few hundred feet under some linden trees. They close themselves off from the world, and in particular from the world of action, which is one form of culture. A science of action exists, one that helps us manage and shape everyday life.

Elie Wiesel: You have always been sensitive to matters involving art, and at the same time you have been a man of action. Did aesthetics influence your actions?

François Mitterrand: Many world leaders ignore the aesthetic dimension; others are drawn to it, believing that an aesthetic sensibility will help them to govern better and to contribute more to the progress of the society over which they hold responsibility. In all modesty, I placed myself among the latter. Was it useful to me in the exercise of my duties? Yes, I believe so. Whatever enabled me to step back without at the same time forcing me to sever my connections to people and things was, it seemed to me, indispensable to action. Separating one part of our selves from other parts, creating a distance between ourselves and others and between thought and action, permits us to observe the general outlines of matters that would otherwise be incomprehensible. The trickiest part is finding the right balance. The success of any action depends on it.

Elie Wiesel: Yet you also write.

François Mitterrand: I write when I am not absorbed by my public life. It is impossible to write — and this you must know better than anyone — without that spiritual unity that only temporal unity makes possible. Having to act most often prevented me from finding sufficient inner serenity. Forcing thoughts to paper requires time. Fatigue, the accumulative weight of responsibilities, and too much energy expended doing other things — all these conspired to make it difficult for me to disengage. There is a time for doing and a time for writing, though sometimes it is possible to combine them in occasional works, such as speeches, memos, prefaces.

Elie Wiesel: For me — and I think this feeling is shared — writing begins in mystery. Words surge forth and what a writer does is align them, channel them, guide them. Why, I wonder, did this word come to me rather than some other?

François Mitterrand: One doesn't start to write without knowing what one wants to say. But how we say something, and what unexpected subjects we find ourselves exploring — this is very mysterious, you are right. Doubtless the process is linked to workings of the brain, to intelligence, to sensibility, and to familiarity.

Elie Wiesel: Put another way, sometimes you surprise yourself.

François Mitterrand: I am indeed often surprised by what I have produced. When I think it's bad, I start over. Most of the time I'm dissatisfied with what I've done, and this means I really have to work at it.

Elie Wiesel: Which is the most difficult — starting or starting over?

François Mitterrand: Starting. Once you're underway, once you're launched, writing can sometimes become a pleasure and always becomes a need. What excuses I've come up with at the very moment I begin work on a book (I've written some thirteen or fourteen) just to keep from sitting down at my desk! I'll get distracted by a shelf in my library and before long be wasting my time over some history book or art book. Or my dog will start to bark and I'll have to go outside to see what's going on. As soon as I get outside, I'll want to relax, and so I'll set off for a half-hour walk. Maybe I won't like the pen I'm using. My pigheaded procrastination can last for days. I tend to want the first draft to be perfect, as polished as if I had spent a long time working on it. This means that I can spend four or five extra days reworking the first sentences of my manuscript. I believe that it is better to start off writing clumsily about what you haven't yet fully thought through. This early material has the merit of existing and can prove useful when you get to the point of fine-tuning things. For me the real work begins after I've finished the rough draft. By then I've turned back into an optimist.

Elie Wiesel: The time one invests in a literary work is never wasted.

François Mitterrand: True. When you separate the wheat from the chaff something of value always remains. That said, I don't pretend to be a writer. I know my native language and concentrate on writing it well. I would have devoted my life to writing if I'd been a writer. Public life has absorbed by far the greater part of my energies, so I've never had the chance to do that. I don't know whether Balzac had other occupations aside from being a writer, but when someone such as you asks me about my writing, I'm clear-eyed enough to know where my limits are.

Elie Wiesel: Yet you do write, and I'm wondering whether when you were acting in a public capacity the writer in you wasn't already considering the manner in which what you did would be recorded.

François Mitterrand: Writing my own memoirs interests me less than offering a justification for what I did. I cannot see myself composing volumes devoted to my life and to the events in which I have played a part. On the other hand, I would be tempted to offer my perspective on some of the great issues I have had to face, and by so doing sketch a self-portrait through my actions. Still, what preoccupies me even more than the opinions of my contemporaries are those future historians will hold. I am not haunted by History, despite what some of my biographers write. Nor am I insensitive to it. This seems to me a useful distinction. If I was to govern France within the context of Europe, to perceive France's future in relation to the development of these countries, it was important for me to learn as much as I could about the history of these other countries. My own role in that history tells me little.

Elie Wiesel: Do you read what others write about you?

François Mitterrand: It isn't one of my obsessions. The books arrive on my desk without my having to go look for them. I sometimes open one or two, but rarely.

Elie Wiesel: At first I told myself I didn't need to read what was written about me. Either it would be nice and I would be flattered, or it would wound me and cause me pain. I've also stopped reading reviews. Are you sensitive to criticism?

François Mitterrand: Yes, though whatever pain or irritation I might experience, whatever sadness I feel at having been misunderstood, doesn't last long. What I find hardest to take is that sense of injustice I feel when I'm made to mean things I didn't mean. Having my actions misinterpreted can enrage me as well as ruffle my vanity.

Elie Wiesel: Have you ever been tempted to respond to criticism you believed was unfounded?

François Mitterrand: Not really. In any case, I never have.

Elie Wiesel: Can you give me a definition of literature?

François Mitterrand: Writing earns the fair name of literature when certain properties of language, style, and form contribute to an overall effect. I won't surprise you by saying that I believe there are many kinds of literature. I personally don't feel drawn to writing fiction, though I am an avid reader of it.

Plenty of writers who might have been great mistook their genre. They stubbornly wrote tragedies when they should have written novels, or comedies when they should have written tragedies, or tales and fables when they should have written philosophical essays. They have squandered their destiny by choosing the wrong approach. The truly great writers have instinctively found the style and format that best served their talents.

Elie Wiesel: Which have served you best?

François Mitterrand: Though I am miserly about my secrets I am fond of relating my own experience from carefully chosen perspectives, and of projecting my own reflection onto the backdrop of the history I lived through. Political commentary and essays are most appropriate for this. When I write I try to provide my reactions to History as I see it, mixing together my sensibilities and personal experiences, my grasp of events. A hill, a river, some trees lining the river, a certain light in the sky — these tell me as much about France as a debate between Clemenceau and Poincaré,[18] and with as much force.

Elie Wiesel: In one of your books you wrote thirty pages that are nearly autobiographical in nature.

François Mitterrand: True. I wanted to show as precisely as I could who my family was and what my childhood was like. To

[18] Though Georges Clemenceau (1841–1929) was never elected president of France, he was one of its most dominant politicians in the twentieth century, and a staunch opponent of right-wing conservatism. His long-time adversary President Raymond Poincaré (1860–1934) appointed him prime minister in 1917 to help restore faith in the government.

my way of thinking, precision is absolutely vital to literature. Being precise doesn't always mean finding the *mot juste.* The mystery and murkiness of *Maldoror's Songs*[19] provide a good example. Even if the narrative appears to stray from the norms of thought or feeling, words stick in a precise way to both. No work of literature can achieve anything more beautiful than that. The writer must say that a stone is flat when it is flat. If a mineral has a certain color, he must say which color — same for an animal or plant of whatever name. That was why I was so taken by the *Nouveau Roman.*[20] The plots are generally not very exciting and everything is called by its name. There is no pretension. Excessively fussy and overly elaborate language can lead to an off-putting abstruseness. I detest writers who insist on using obscure words, words that are precious and allusive and correspond to a particular moment in linguistic history — but which are imprecise insofar as their current usage.

Elie Wiesel: Words that are precious today weren't precious two centuries ago.

François Mitterrand: Philology — the history of words — is a fascinating science and one I am passionate about. I like knowing if such and such a word derives from Latin, or that

[19] Controversial and eccentric, *Maldoror's Songs* (full French title, *Les Chants de Maldoror par le comte de Lautréamont*) were originally published in Belgium in 1869 because they were banned in France. Written by Isidore Ducasse, they were later championed by the surrealists as heralding the beginning of modern literature in France.

[20] Literary movement of the 1950s and 1960s (literally meaning "New Novel") typified by the works of Alain Robbe-Grillet, Michel Butor, and Claude Simon, among others.

another has Celtic roots, or that a third dates from the period of the Teutonic invasions. The meanings of words change over the course of their history. Even if it isn't what I would call literature, I find it amusing to take sixteenth-century dialogue or description and rephrase it, using only words that people today would employ.

Elie Wiesel: Are you a purist when it comes to language?

François Mitterrand: I like it when words are used exactly as they were during a given historical period. That doesn't mean that from time to time you shouldn't indulge in an anachronism, a bold turn of phrase, words in English or in "Franglais," or slang. Some who have been masters of slang have written at a very sophisticated level.

Elie Wiesel: You studied Latin, history, and the humanities. Were these useful in the development of your mind? What influence did Cicero have on your speaking style, for example, or Tacitus on your speaking abilities?

François Mitterrand: Yes. I loved Latin very much — which has contributed to the evolution, or devolution, of my style — so much so that I deplore the fact that Latin is so little taught these days. The rhythms of French resemble those of Latin and a number of French words contain Latin roots. Any language is impoverished when disconnected from its origins. I know it is very difficult to teach a subject that seems impractical to so many children, but you have asked about me and that is how I feel. I was good at French, history, geography. I was not very good at Latin. My translations tended to be a little free-wheeling and I had trouble with the assignments. On the other hand, I reveled in the language, memorizing whole passages of Horace and Virgil by heart and taking them apart according to the nearly mechanical Latin metrics. I ruined all my textbooks by marking them up with slashes and lines indicating meter. I spent entire evenings doing this just for fun. I repeated the meter of the Latin verse without always really understanding it.

Elie Wiesel: Do your speeches today reflect this?

François Mitterrand: Possibly.

Elie Wiesel: Giacometti had a lovely phrase: "My dream," he said, "is to sculpt a bust so small that I can put it in a box of matches, which will then be so heavy no one can lift it." Isn't that also true for a book? Every book should be so dense, so real, and so pure that it fits into the palm of your hand.

François Mitterrand: I am often accused of having an exaggerated taste for Chardonne — it is true that in his very French conciseness he had magnificent style. But I enjoy Tolstoy's profusion as much. Tolstoy didn't try to make every page of *War and Peace* weigh two hundred tons, and yet it is still a weighty book.

Elie Wiesel: People normally talk about Tolstoy and Dostoyevski as complete opposites.

François Mitterrand: Forty years ago, when I was asked what book I thought was the most beautiful book I had ever read I replied, "*The Brothers Karamazov.*" Today, I prefer works by Tolstoy.

Elie Wiesel: To return to writing proper, I know that for me the most difficult moment is the one that precedes the moment

I begin to write. Why? Because if I can get the first sentence right then I have the first page, and the whole book. Is it the same for you?

François Mitterrand: It is true that with the first sentence I too have the feeling of being underway, of having won the battle. Nonetheless, even if it contains a beautiful image, I wouldn't go so far as to say that this first sentence contains the first page, and that in turn the first page contains the whole book. Perhaps because I am not a professional writer. Though often when I read I get the feel of a book from its first line, from its music, its thought, most especially its verve.

Elie Wiesel: I knew a Yiddish writer once who considered himself a prince among writers. He was a grand fellow, very influential, and wrote in both Hebrew and Yiddish. I was very young when I met him and he said to me, "Young man, one day you will write. What is a writer but a coachman driving a carriage? And what does a coachman do when he arrives in a town? He cracks the whip so that everyone knows he has arrived. What else does he do? He cracks it again so that everyone knows when he's leaving. Between these two moments, he can do as he wishes and go where he pleases. It is the same thing for a book: the first and last crack of the whip are important. In between, everything is possible." His words have always stayed with me. What's important is to have the final word. It carries all the others that have gone before it.

François Mitterrand: The crack of the whip doesn't only warn the people in the town, it warns the horse, and the horse is more useful than either the whip or the coachman. First it won't budge and then it won't halt. What is terrible, I find, is that there is always something more to be said, something to add, something that might have been put better.

Elie Wiesel: I know a wonderful story about a horse. One day, a woman called me to invite me to give a reading. In the course of our conversation I began to wonder if a mistake hadn't been made, because she didn't seem to have read a single one of my books. "I'll put her audience to the test," I told myself. We agreed that I would read from one of my books. But instead I made up a completely different story, one that had nothing whatever to do with that novel — I changed the time and turned my characters into caricatures. I was sure that someone in the auditorium would stand up and interrupt me, saying, "But that isn't the novel we read." But everyone at the reading listened attentively. When I'd finished, the woman who'd arranged everything and who presided over the event asked if there were any questions. A few hands went up. I told myself, "Aha! Now someone's going to react." Well, the questions they asked were about the novel I had fabricated. "We read your novel," they said, "and it's magnificent." Then several talked about this story that I had just told as if it really were part of my novel.

Afterward I took the woman who'd invited me aside and told her the following story: A rabbi is supposed to attend a religious ceremony in another village. He goes to a coachman whose carriage is pulled by a sickly-looking, swaybacked old horse and asks the coachman to take him. Outside town they come to a hill. The coachman stops the carriage and says to the rabbi, "My horse is too weak to pull the carriage. Let's get out and push." So the rabbi gets out and he and the coachman push the carriage, and together they manage to get it over the hill. They continue to push until they arrive at the village where the rabbi is supposed to be. The rabbi turns to the coachman and says, "I know why you're here — you have to make money. I know why I'm here — I was invited to a ceremony. There's one thing I don't understand. Why did we bring the horse?" I sometimes have the same feeling about my books.

Certain writers write from adoration. Others from rage. For myself, I wanted to testify to what I owed to my people and to their history. Gratitude is a cardinal virtue in life and in literature.

François Mitterrand: For me, testifying was not what was essential. I too felt the desire to do so, of course, but it was secondary. First books are often born of an impulse and mine sprang from a need to explain my life and times to my contemporaries. I wanted to wrestle with the whole host of issues surrounding decolonialization, and to use those issues as a means of demonstrating, proving, and persuading.

Elie Wiesel: From what perspective?

François Mitterrand: A political perspective. I was trying to understand the whole chain of events by tracing the passions of men in my time.

Elie Wiesel: You became a writer in order to persuade people. But you were also an important speaker. Which has served you better in achieving your aims? The written word or the spoken word?

François Mitterrand: If I have not always convinced everyone, at least I have enlarged the circle of those who are moved by the same issues as I. I have written far less than spoken, doubtless because there is an immense gulf between thinking and writing, and speaking seems the easier of the two. Between the moment when we are struck by the impulse to write and when we actually sit down to write, thought stiffens. Things clot and lose their urgency. The whole challenge lies in recapturing that urgency through work and reflection. Serenity alone makes it possible, peace with oneself.

Elie Wiesel: There speaks the voice of the creator.

François Mitterrand: I wouldn't use that exact term. True creators invent worlds and new systems of thought. Because it gives form to the formless, the written text is of course an act of creation, but there are many degrees of separation between amoebas and humans. As far as writing goes, I am closer to the amoeba.

Elie Wiesel: Have you ever wanted to write a work of fiction?

François Mitterrand: Gathering together certain experiences, certain scenes from my life that carry a moral, and putting them into a brief narrative would be tempting. Constructing a fictional literary work around it, one in which the imagination plays an important role? No, I have never wanted to.

Elie Wiesel: There is a very beautiful and troubling fable about Moses being given the power to travel ahead in time. He travels two thousand years ahead and goes to listen to the teachings of an expert on the Torah. When the lesson is over Moses departs, feeling crushed. He understood not one of the man's explanations, despite the fact that it was his own Book under discussion. I think the same thing happens to all writers. You sometimes read reviews of which you are the subject and still you understand absolutely nothing. So if you seek to convince, it's because your project contains a message you want to get across.

François Mitterrand: Ordinarily a writer's fame stems from his mastery of language. His existence can become precarious if the kind of writing he champions doesn't conform to mainstream tastes, in which case he can become either a high priest or a pariah.

Elie Wiesel: Might it not be the role of the writer to be an outcast?

François Mitterrand: There have been many official writers, as well a number of others who, once they were established, could never be outcasts. Victor Hugo may have been exiled but he was never a pariah.

Elie Wiesel: Hugo was a writer of best-sellers. A hundred thousand copies of his books of poems were sold! His writing drew its power from the community in which he lived and worked as a public figure. For others, by contrast, fighting City Hall is a precondition of writing.

François Mitterrand: There are so many branches to literature that it seems difficult to apply one general rule.

Elie Wiesel: What are your preferences?

François Mitterrand: I am very eclectic in my reading. When I was twenty, I was attracted to the literature of action, of which Malraux was the prototype. Later I realized that it was all pasteboard: a false witness recounting false actions.

Elie Wiesel: Malraux was nonetheless a great writer! There is a Malraux voice, a Malraux universe.

François Mitterrand: An exceptional man, certainly. A great writer? That's open to debate. *The Human Condition* marked a generation, but it's already dated. *Man's Hope,* on the other hand, has left a more enduring legacy. Still, even if it carries a message, I would hope my writing might convince my reader of the beauty and reality of a landscape, capturing and communicating by describing the essence of what I myself perceive.

Elie Wiesel: When you reread something you've written do you have the feeling of having captured that beauty?

François Mitterrand: I have occasionally had that feeling. When I write, a sort of sixth sense tells me when I'm going off track. I only publish works that I feel I have finished.

Elie Wiesel: What was the first novel you ever read?

François Mitterrand: I couldn't give you a precise reply. The library in the house where I grew up contained works by the great authors of the second half of the nineteenth century — there were few novels by Zola but plenty by Paul Bourget. I must have started by reading authors whose works were readily available: Balzac, Stendhal, Flaubert. During the 1930s, my choice was guided by what the *Nouvelle revue française* published, introducing me to the works of Gide, Montherlant, Bernanos, Claudel, Mauriac, Drieu la Rochelle.[21]

Elie Wiesel: Do you honestly not have a preference for certain kinds of literature over others?

François Mitterrand: I'm sure I do, but I read whatever I happen to find, or whatever — for reasons I often don't understand — strikes a chord in me, either because the book looks nice, or because I find the typography pleasing, or else because while flipping through the book I find an arresting image or turn of phrase. I read haphazardly, my choices dictated by impulse. I often come out of a bookstore carrying something I had no intention of buying when I went in.

Elie Wiesel: What else have you read?

François Mitterrand: In my youth, when the fashion was for English novels, I read Rosamonde Lehmann and Charles Morgan. Later I discovered Faulkner and Hemingway. Later still — and better still — Joyce. I also have a weakness for Sty-

---

[21] Paul Bourget (1852–1935), poet and novelist, was the author of *The Disciple,* an attack on Ernest Renan's views of the roles of intellectuals in society. Henry de Montherlant's 1941 novel *The June Solstice,* published during the German occupation, was pointedly collaborationist. Paul Claudel (1868–1955) is best known for his plays, which include *Break at Noon* and *The Satin Slipper.* Pierre Drieu la Rochelle (1894–1945), French Fascist and intellectual, was the author of the autobiographical novel *Gilles* (1939).

ron.[22] At the same time, however, I was devouring Balzac, Stendhal, Flaubert, Chateaubriand, and, again, anything I could find on the shelves of my family's library.

Elie Wiesel: Outside of religious books, in which I was steeped, certain books marked me. Those by Kafka, to whom I feel extremely close — so close that I believe that there is the world before Kafka, and the world after Kafka. Books by Dostoyevski, same thing.

François Mitterrand: Another book that stands in opposition to *The Brothers Karamazov* in terms of style, breadth, and subject is *Strait Is the Gate* by André Gide.

Elie Wiesel: How about *The Castle*? I remember clearly the first time I read Kafka. It was at night. When I heard the garbage collectors in the street early the next morning I wanted to go out and shake their hands, to thank them for having reminded me with their racket that another world besides Kafka's existed. Kafka himself was convinced he wrote comedies. When he read his novels to his friends he had fits of laughter. Yet are any books more tragic than his? His dream was to go to Palestine and find work as a waiter in a café. His last words were to his doctor. "If you don't kill me," he told him, "you're a murderer."

François Mitterrand: Was he in as much pain as that?

---

[22] Rosamonde Lehmann (born 1901) is a British novelist and short-story writer whose works include *Invitation to the Waltz* (1932) and *The Weather in the Streets* (1936). William Styron, the American writer, is the author of *The Confessions of Nat Turner* and *Sophie's Choice*, among other works.

Elie Wiesel: He had tuberculosis. Death took him when he was still young. Did you know that he wrote to his sister every day? And that in not one of his letters does he even mention the war? Kafka was one of the great witnesses of this century. He was there when the war started in 1914 and he saw the wounded — yet not so much as one word about any of that in his letters. Writers today bear a heavier responsibility. No longer can we write with impunity anything we want, the way we could before.

François Mitterrand: Perhaps, but remember that from time immemorial even activist writers have submitted to events. The ones who were shot in 1945 were writers — not those who helped construct the Atlantic Wall.[23] An intellectual bears more responsibility than a financier or an entrepreneur.

Elie Wiesel: Writers were also the ones executed in the former Soviet Union before 1936, or in 1952.

François Mitterrand: There is nothing new in this. Cicero and Seneca — to cite just two examples — were driven to suicide.

Elie Wiesel: For the Romans suicide was a sort of custom. Despite the fact that Socrates could have chosen exile, the example of his death seems more appropriate.

François Mitterrand: They had all expressed nonconformist ideas. The writer runs risks when he writes.

---

[23] Fortifications built by the Germans (with French labor) along the Atlantic Coast to repel an Allied invasion.

Elie Wiesel: As a writer, have you had the same impression I have sometimes had, that what was most important was left unsaid?

François Mitterrand: If the gist of what I wanted to say has not been said I keep working at it. Given my expectations, I have never felt regret about my books. To say anything of the sort requires a presumption I do not have.

Elie Wiesel: I have written nearly thirty books and often had the impression of not having even started.

François Mitterrand: That is surely because you are far more demanding than I am. Still, if you seek an explanation from the world there is every chance you will die disappointed.

Elie Wiesel: That depends entirely on who is standing over my shoulders, reading. What part does silence play in your writing?

François Mitterrand: It is a good complement, an inner necessity, secondary to what is outside. To write one must create for oneself an inner unity around silence. There can be noise outside — that isn't disruptive — but it is impossible to write if one is buffeted by too many inner conflicts.

Elie Wiesel: Do you see silence as the opposite of words?

François Mitterrand: No, they are complementary.

Elie Wiesel: Can they contain silence?

François Mitterrand: Yes. There have to be breathing spaces. Silence gives the reader time to orient himself and to reflect.

Elie Wiesel: Do you think French literature is healthy at this moment?

François Mitterrand: On the whole, yes, though not fiction. Few contemporary novelists can boast the universality of a Fernand Braudel or a Claude Lévi-Strauss.

Elie Wiesel: What writers do you personally admire?

François Mitterrand: Very few who write about politics. More so those whose fields are art, spirituality, and philosophy.

Elie Wiesel: Why make a distinction between the artist and politics? The cultural world is beset by as much jealousy and rancor, as many crises, as the political world. It is just as much a world of power.

François Mitterrand: I know the political world better than the artistic.

Elie Wiesel: What is it about the artistic world that you admire? The creative power?

François Mitterrand: Yes, the power of a painter to create a painting, or a composer a symphony. A piece of sculpture, a system of thought capable of lifting the senses and the intellect beyond their limits — to me these are almost magic.

Elie Wiesel: The painter paints and the musician composes, yet how many readers does a novelist today have, and a composer how many listeners? Very few, when all is said and done. Whereas politicians work for millions of men and women. Why not recognize this creative dimension in politics? You personally have accorded culture a preeminent role and initiated the construction of huge projects such as the Louvre, the Bastille opera, the Arc de la Défense, and above all, France's national library.

François Mitterrand: Quite true. I have tried to make sure these projects were of major significance. But that is part of my public responsibility; or at least as I see it. The creative dimension of that responsibility has guided my actions and in any case infused them with a poetry I do not always find in the law.

V

POWER

Elie Wiesel: Power fascinates us. Why do we seek it? What does it bring us? What are its purposes and its traps? What definition would you give it?

François Mitterrand: The dictionary definition. We should keep sight of the essential — that power can assume a thousand forms. That it can extend into the private life, reaching right into the heart of the family structure. That it can be found in city halls, in villages and megalopolises nationwide. That it can also be produced by the mind through teaching, writing, and the arts. Power will always mean the capacity accorded to an individual or a group of individuals to impress their will and their vision onto a far larger collective, and to guide its destiny.

Elie Wiesel: Does it mean the superiority of one individual over others?

François Mitterrand: I would say instead that exercising power requires a particular talent. Is it a mark of superiority? Those who exercise power are not necessarily better than others; they simply have more aptitude for it. It is purely a question of capacity.

Elie Wiesel: What gives the powerful their power?

François Mitterrand: With regard to teaching, writing, and the arts, as I said, it involves mental gifts, the ability to express at a particular moment in time people's unexpressed feelings and unexpressed needs. With regard to social organization, whoever is in power controls the levers governing the bureaucracy — and to do so he has received the electoral benediction of a democratic system.

Elie Wiesel: Is the power of an artist — Goethe or Goya, for example — comparable to that of a president?

François Mitterrand: They represent different forms of power. If you want to establish a hierarchy of these forms, at the very top is the power wielded solely by the imagination and what it can create. After that come forms of power that are more immediate and visible — political, economic, or social.

Elie Wiesel: Those powers we recognize.

François Mitterrand: The power of miracle workers and opinion makers is mysterious. In the Middle Ages, Vincent Ferrier, Abelard, or Bernard attracted enormous crowds. So did, much later, Gambetta, Jaurès, and Lenin.[24]

Elie Wiesel: Doesn't power consist in part of illusion?

---

[24] Vincent Ferrier was a fifteenth-century Spanish clergymen whose lifework was an attempt to mend the Western Schism. Peter Abelard (1079–1142) was a philosopher and popular teacher at the University of Paris. Bernard de Clairvaux (1091–1153) was a powerful clergyman and Templar who opposed Abelard's rationalism. He was later sainted. Léon Gambetta (1838–1882) and Jean Jaurès (1859–1914) were French socialists and active politicians. Jaurès founded the French Socialist party in 1905.

François Mitterrand: Political power resides not in the illusions it creates but in the hopes it incarnates — hopes that can themselves be illusory. The illusion of power is a philosophical notion. Compared to an individual's fate, power is a paltry thing. One thing is certain, however, and that is that power is not illusory when in the hands of those who would use it to exalt themselves or to destroy a people. Power is always fearsome, I believe, and if those who have it are not afraid of it they should at least be extraordinarily vigilant about its nature and reach. If they are wise they will themselves seek ways to keep it in check. When one submits to power one tries to find ways of controlling its excesses. That is why political philosophy has, little by little, turned toward a concept of a democracy in action, separating powers in order to control them and decentralizing them in order to distribute them more evenly. In the financial and social arenas, for example, unions act as an important counterbalance to power. So too in art what is sometimes necessary is to break through conformity and break down the power of convention, giving rise to new schools of thought, new standards and styles of expression.

Elie Wiesel: What, therefore, is true power?

François Mitterrand: The answer lies in history. I am thinking of those great radicals like Etienne Marcel[25] or Spartacus, whom the establishment defeated, and of others like Lenin, who swept it away. The powers-that-were viewed

---

[25] Etienne Marcel (1315–1358), also known as the "master of Paris," sided with the Navarre kings in their opposition to Charles V and promised to deliver Paris to the Navarre cause.

Christ himself as a rabble-rouser; their view killed him. His revenge has been posthumous — in the form of the church that was founded upon his teachings. No one could argue that its power was insignificant. Not bad for a small-time trouble-maker from the provinces. It was believed he had lost, but in the end he won.

Elie Wiesel: I am reminded of Moses and Socrates.

François Mitterrand: Unlike most agitators, neither Socrates nor Christ sought political power. They contented themselves with an idea, a project, a morality, a sacrifice. Yet an institution was born of Christ's teachings, an institution whose later adherents used it to assume power. Socrates kept strictly to the realm of thought.

Elie Wiesel: The source of Socrates' power is Plato. I was talking about the power of the individual — that of the priest, prophet, or king. Of the three the prophet would seem the most subversive, the most individualistic, because he represents nothing. He is supported neither by the people nor by the king, and all that remains of his life is his word.

François Mitterrand: People sometimes side with the prophet.

Elie Wiesel: Do you think political power needs to be kept in check?

François Mitterrand: Without question. If there must be real power over a given society, there must also exist forces that balance — not destroy — its extent. Man will always test the limits of his power, whether that power be executive, legislative, judicial, or journalistic. Achieving a just balance means finding safeguards.

Elie Wiesel: What you have written about your experience in the camps during World War II moved me deeply. In particular you mention a man, a German carpenter from Thuringe, who suddenly found himself your keeper. He possessed power over you.

François Mitterrand: In a manner of speaking, I was like a slave whose muscles are measured on the auction block. Without necessarily looking at me as if I were a slave, the carpenter singled me out from among the others. To tell the truth, I didn't find it unpleasant to be marched off by armed guards each day and taken to a workshop that smelled of wood and sawdust and echoed with the noise of machines. My great grandfather had been a wood dealer and the sights and sounds of the woodshop were in my blood. The carpenter had enormously long, flat pencils he used to measure lengths and to indicate where the pieces needed to be cut. He was a good man. He treated me more as a colleague than a laborer. He was obsessed by Napoléon, I remember, and when he penciled something for me on a plank of wood, he would also mark down the dates of the battles of Austerlitz or Iéna, or the wedding day of Maria-Louise. In his quarters was an enormous collection of photographs he had haphazardly clipped from newspapers and magazines.

Elie Wiesel: Despite his kindness, didn't you experience a feeling of powerlessness?

François Mitterrand: The carpenter's power over me was the least of my worries. During March 1941, I felt terribly isolated and sorry for myself. I would say to myself, "Here it is 1941, and I'm locked away in a cell in a medieval prison in the heart of Germany under the dictatorship of a man who rules Europe and who boasts" — the Russians hadn't yet entered the war — "that his Europe will endure for a thousand years. My family has no idea where I am and the army I was a soldier in has completely lost sight of me. My former comrades-in-arms have also disappeared. Apart from my jailer and maybe a guard or two, no one in the village knows I even exist." The only thing I had to read was a missal that had belonged to an escapee. He had been my one social contact. I read the psalms to pass the time and to force me to remember my Latin.

I had never known such loneliness and isolation, and it seemed all the worse because there was nothing to indicate that it wouldn't go on like that for the rest of my life.

There were also moments when I felt confident. One of our greatest weaknesses lies in how we imagine the future. We inevitably see it in terms of the present. Sometimes we do so for noble reasons — as in the case of grief or sorrow, when we focus our pain on the thought that one day that pain will diminish. We know instinctively that happiness is fleeting. But consider another situation, like a setback in the career you've chosen, for example. You feel discredited, shunted aside. You believe this setback is irreversible and you wallow in self-pity. Yet actually life is all-powerful, and the following day, the week after that, or — for those who are patient — a year or two later, the pieces in the puzzle change. You might say that I'm an optimist. I have never believed that any obstacle was insurmountable.

We should not give in to our conservative nature and

become engrossed by what we find in the present. We should place more confidence in our instincts, and in life's extraordinary capacity to change — and, as a consequence, to change us.

Elie Wiesel: For me, it is the past I find I'm unable to imagine.

François Mitterrand: Yours has been clouded by blood and death, marked by moments of terror. This is a particular phenomenon millions like yourself have experienced, but which the vast majority of humanity has not. I myself was spared. Therefore I cannot have the same reactions to the past that you have.

Elie Wiesel: You spoke of the extreme loneliness you felt when you thought the outside world had forgotten you. We too have felt forgotten. I was convinced that I would not survive the war, and that once I had been deported to that place I would not come out alive. But I would like us to go back to power, and in particular to its limits. God has the absolute power and yet according to the New Testament He Himself imposes limits upon it. How does that compare to man?

François Mitterrand: Let's leave aside creative power — that of the individual sitting alone at his desk — for it is impossible for me to argue that some genius, suddenly realizing that he was using his gifts for evil, would voluntarily make mistakes in syntax! One cannot entrust man with the responsibility of limiting his own power. Society must see to it that its mechanisms are designed to give significant power to those it calls upon to speak and act in its name, but also with internal checks and balances. Society can only survive by institutionalizing itself. Freedoms cannot withstand anarchy or even simple majority will. Once institutionalized, a hierarchy of power — political, union, business, cultural, media — gets put in place, and if the whole edifice has been constructed intelligently, it will be steadied by the play of checks and balances. Human history bears this out. There will be periodic shifts in favor of one side or another, but because of the very nature of the institution these powers will equalize. That is why I believe in the usefulness of lawyers. Of course, as president of France, some of my powers were more than just matters of conscience — these included the power to give clemency, to decide whether or not to use nuclear force, whether or not to dissolve the National Assembly, and so forth. The responsibility for these lay on my shoulders alone. Whatever decision I came to emerged after long inner debate and was final. No one could do it for me, nor even offer help.

Elie Wiesel: Can the conscience of a head of state impose its own limits?

François Mitterrand: I know of only two limiting powers: popular vote and a sense of duty.

Elie Wiesel: Why does creative power not follow the same rules?

François Mitterrand: Because it is different in its very nature. Why limit the power of a philosopher, for example?

Elie Wiesel: Nonetheless that is what I do. There are things I will not say and things I will not write.

François Mitterrand: When an individual engages in internal debate, his conscience alone acts as a restraint. There it is a question of moral control. As soon as we begin to talk about individual power, power carried by the channels of the imagination, we must understand that only the individual possesses the ability to decide what limits are not to be exceeded. Imposed from outside, those limits represent censorship, and that is a far greater evil.

Elie Wiesel: You say institutions must guarantee that no tyrant can impose his own law. How do you recognize that particular moment when power devolves into tyranny?

François Mitterrand: One judges power by its deeds. Until the birth of democracy and its recent progress, their way of life in society led people to endow one person with absolute power.

Elie Wiesel: Is there a difference, in either degree or substance, between absolute power held by one individual and power residing in the hands of a group of individuals?

François Mitterrand: No. They are of the same nature, whether a political party, a church, a clan, or an ethnic group. Moreover, these groups generally submit themselves to an internal power often embodied in one individual. Rarely is this not the case: the Venice Ten[26] serve as a good model for collective decision-making.

Elie Wiesel: If power is judged by its deeds, there must be good deeds and bad, the good ones being the ones the people accept.

---

[26] The Venice Ten, also known as the Council of Ten, consisted of ten men chosen in secrecy by Venice's Grand Council in the fourteenth century and given absolute power to maintain order in Venice.

François Mitterrand: You cannot predict whether an act will bring either good or ill. All you can do is wait for its effects and then decide whether it has increased mankind's sufferings, or whether, by creating conditions of greater joy, liberty, stability, thought, and understanding, it has alleviated suffering. We have no criteria by which to judge power other than by its effects. When institutions encourage crime, they must be reformed. Absolute rulers can have good intentions when they first ascend to power, but they all end by losing sight of the limits of their power and therefore by committing arbitrary acts.

Elie Wiesel: I am thinking about the post you occupied in 1944 following the liberation of Paris. You were secretary general for prisoners of war and that meant you had power.

François Mitterrand: I was part of a team charged with maintaining governmental legitimacy, in theory throughout France but in reality in Paris and a few of the liberated provinces. What power I had was delegated to me. All the real decisions fell to General de Gaulle and the Committee for the Liberation of Algeria.[27] But since we were physically separated from them, we were forced to improvise, to make our own decisions. We didn't do that for very long.

Elie Wiesel: Was it in any way analogous to the power you wielded when you were president of France?

---

[27] The Committee for the Liberation of Algeria, also known as the French Committee of National Liberty, was the body directing the wartime efforts of the French government-in-exile. After 1943, it was led by General de Gaulle.

François Mitterrand: No. There were fifteen of us and I was the youngest and without question the least influential. I didn't even communicate directly with de Gaulle and Algeria. In 1981, the power given to me by the French people was really mine alone.

Elie Wiesel: Were you prepared to assume this power?

François Mitterrand: Yes. I had spent thirty-five years in politics and had been in government for seven of those years, during which time I learned what sort of decisions needed to be made. And for twenty-four years I was a member of the opposition party. This enabled me to reflect long and hard upon what I would do if I came to power, and what sort of people I would choose to help me.

Elie Wiesel: Did all the years you spent in the opposition leave their mark on you?

François Mitterrand: You learn to appreciate your role. I could have stayed there without complaint, and since it seemed so completely unlikely that things would ever turn around there was no need to learn resignation. That's just how things were. I would have wanted to have a voice people listened to regardless of whether or not I made it to power.

Elie Wiesel: Did your political defeats leave you depressed?

François Mitterrand: No, never. My whole party was in defeat. To ever succeed in bringing it to victory was a risky proposition. The commentators could dismiss me by saying I always lost, but that meant nothing. It took Léon Blum's

Popular Front fifteen years to triumph. It took me ten years — from the creation of the socialist party in 1971 to my election in 1981. Between these two dates seemed like little else than a string of defeats. Actually, we were making constant progress.

Elie Wiesel: Did the reality of power correspond with what you had imagined?

François Mitterrand: I had come close enough to formulate a fairly accurate notion of what it would mean, though I think I underestimated it. Since 1958, the president of France — so long as he has maintained the consent of the people — has been given wide-ranging powers.[28] His only limits are internal. I have voluntarily limited my own power. Sometimes it is wisest to listen to what an institution is telling you rather than rely solely on your own judgment.

Elie Wiesel: True power, therefore, is the power that one exercises over oneself. Didn't you have your share of heartbreak and exultation?

François Mitterrand: If anyone in a position of power allows himself to wallow in self-pity he will live in a state of constant uncertainty. It is a noble thing to agonize over the consequences of a decision, but it can turn into a permanent contradiction. What is important is to be aware of risk. When I exulted in my power it was because it gave me the ability to

---

[28] When de Gaulle was elected president of France in 1958, beginning the Fifth Republic, he considerably expanded the power and prestige of the office.

realize my aspirations — to take the country in the direction I believed guaranteed its security, the well-being of its citizens, and greater justice for certain social groups. But you also cannot live in a perpetual state of euphoria. One day you rejoice because you've done something that will bring good to the greater number of people. The next day life reminds you that responsibility is not about that. Some of Pierre Mauroy's great governmental reforms delighted me, but I learned not to depend on that feeling.[29] Each hour of every day taught me something that pulled me out of that state of innocence.

Elie Wiesel: What lives on after a person dies are his actions, and his words as well. History will judge your actions. I want to know how you yourself judge them.

François Mitterrand: Being by nature dissatisfied, I believe my achievements fall well below my ambitions. In a general way, I agree with the criticisms made of me — though my enemies are wrong to condemn wholesale everything I have done. My own self-criticism is mitigated, naturally enough. I think it unfair to denigrate everything I've done. In any case, if someday someone is so inclined they will find in my words and writings, and in my actions, something that will nourish their faith in the future of humanity, in France's future, and in Europe's progress, and find that they share some of my ideals and morals.

---

[29] Pierre Mauroy was appointed prime minister by François Mitterrand in 1981 and served until 1984.

Elie Wiesel: What makes you feel most proud? To have accomplished something, to have made crowds come to life, to have inspired enthusiasm? Or are you most proud of being able to say: "I lost at that, yet I did not lose myself?"

François Mitterrand: I am most proud of some things I have written, and of some accomplishments: banishing the death penalty, forging France's new identity after decentralization, defending at certain critical moments the oppressed people of the Third World, influencing the development of Europe. I believe they are all part of an agenda I could be proud of, were I inclined to feel pride.

Elie Wiesel: In other words, you have sought to reunite people and principles.

François Mitterrand: Yes, at least I have tried to.

Elie Wiesel: That the outsider not feel like a stranger, nor the defenseless within a community feel unprotected.

François Mitterrand: My inclinations are internationalist in nature. If my country finds itself in danger, however, I act as a patriot.

Elie Wiesel: Do you have any regrets?

François Mitterrand: Yes, I regret not having done everything I could have done. About unemployment, for example. I know full well this affliction is not peculiar to the French, but France endures it and suffers from it. I have sometimes miscalculated how sluggishly society changes and underestimated the weight of its habits. You cannot change society with legislation. Still, there have been decisive changes since I came to power in 1981. Changes in the legal code involving women and their marital, familial, and financial rights, for example. Laws protecting children. Laws assisting the struggle against segregation. I am proud to have played a part in these changes.

VI

SPECIAL MOMENTS

Elie Wiesel: Life is the sum of special moments, each one of which tells us of what was and engenders what is to come. I would like to talk about certain special moments in your life. What are they? The Liberation of France, for example?

François Mitterrand: There are historic moments in which I have been involved, if only indirectly, and which have changed my life and my thinking. To know which they are, all you need to do is add up France's important events between 1936 and today. You mentioned the Liberation. Yes, it is one of the special moments of my life. But there are others that occurred during the war and when I was in the Resistance, such as the day I finally succeeded in escaping. I experienced a powerful feeling of inner liberation that day. Or my first election in 1946. Or when I was reelected to the Senate in 1958, following my only defeat. On the way back to Paris from Nevers, I felt euphoric. And then of course there was my election as president of France in 1981. In my private life, too, I have known joys of this sort, radiant but unmomentous moments, on a terrace in Florence watching the sunset; walking though the back streets of Venice; in Vézelay and Saint-Benoît. I have no shortage of memories! I remember, one day in the Landes, being overwhelmed by a sense of freedom while watching a flock of wild geese fly overhead. I remember their cries and the beauty of their flight.

Elie Wiesel: Let's try to flesh out particular moments, such as the day France was liberated. What was it like?

François Mitterrand: I really experienced the Liberation when Paris was liberated. The war was not yet over, since there were still whole regions of France waiting to be liberated. I was in Paris — a cabinet member of the provisional government — and we were facing difficult times.

Elie Wiesel: Where were you living?

François Mitterrand: At the intersection of Boulevard Saint-Germain and Boulevard Saint-Michel, very close to the place where some of the heaviest fighting was taking place. I rode my bicycle everywhere. You came across Germans and passing tanks, and from time to time you got shot at. That didn't stop people from going shopping. People would be standing in line to buy milk and bread and suddenly someone would open fire. A few were killed. People threw themselves on the floor for a moment, and then . . . life went on. Not far off, in other parts of Paris, you wouldn't even have known that there was fighting. One evening, while a crowd of us waited for General Leclerc at the Hotel de Ville (he finally arrived later), we felt a powerful feeling of excitement.[30] It was the evening of Saint Louis, the king most closely identified with France's greatness. There was

[30] Philippe-Marie de Hautecloque (1902–1947), also known as Leclerc, commanded the Second Armored Division, which liberated Paris in August of 1944 and accepted the surrender of the German garrison there.

something deeply moving about all of us waiting there together, something symbolic and mystical. Like me, you have felt the simple joy of looking at a clear August night sky and watching a shower of shooting stars. I did that often in my childhood, at my grandparents' house, and it gave me a sense of extraordinary fullness. History need not be mixed up in it.

Elie Wiesel: Nonetheless, that day in 1944 was the event, the great event. Paris was liberated, the enemy was defeated and on the run, and you could say that you had something to do with it. What did that victory represent to you? Liberty? The return of something?

François Mitterrand: Not a return but a beginning. Perhaps it was an illusion.

Elie Wiesel: Happiness?

François Mitterrand: A happy event, not happiness. Who knows? I might have had a toothache that day.

Elie Wiesel: But you were not alone. You were with friends.

François Mitterrand: There was a crowd, the people of Paris, and I found being among them very moving. I felt an emotion like the one I felt at certain rallies, or at gatherings with my closest political allies. Seventy thousand, a hundred thousand people, all behaving as if at a classical music concert — that kind of silence that precedes applause.

Elie Wiesel: All the fervor didn't frighten you?

François Mitterrand: I am mindful of the responsibility that falls upon men at moments like that. The evening of my first election to the French presidency, I was in Château-Chinon. It was in May. A storm was rising. I remember running back to the car while the rain came down in sheets. Our car was enveloped by rain and swept by spray and we could only move ahead very slowly. I was elated by what I had accomplished, and by the power I was assuming. At the same time this storm seemed a portent of the difficulties that lay ahead. It proved to be accurate. And it could not have turned out any other way.

Other special moments? An evening during which, very suddenly and without knowing why, you discover friendship, and everyone's heart feels lighter. One day during the Phony War, sometime between 1939 and 1940, I was in a miserable camp among other mud-splattered soldiers. Someone began singing and I found the sound beautiful, and instantly, right there in that grimy, squalid setting, I was filled with excitement for what lay ahead in life, even for the days that would bring neither glory nor happiness.

Elie Wiesel: Because death was so near, death that always hangs in the air during wartime?

François Mitterrand: I didn't think my turn to die had come. I didn't even wonder about it. I was young.

Elie Wiesel: Could you have lived a life other than the one you have lived?

François Mitterrand: I believe so. I could have devoted my life to thought and lived in the country, in the company of trees, animals, and those whom I love. Perhaps this is nothing but a bucolic dream, but I feel as if I could have. The life of the mind, as you know, is as turbulent and as adventurous as a life of action, and to live well I didn't always need change. Still, the spur of action was doubtless sharper than the one of thought, since I eventually threw myself into politics.

Elie Wiesel: We are nearing the end of this century. What do you envision will be the future of the history in which you have played a part?

François Mitterrand: Science and technology will progress, reshuffling the deck and forcing humanity to conceive of a different kind of productive society. Culture will assume an increasingly important place in this society. The absence of faith will give rise to a proliferation of cults. Many will wait for a savior, just as they did in those great medieval tragedies. Let us hope that we will not witness political upheaval of the sort that took place in Germany in 1933.

Elie Wiesel: Would you like to be around to see what happens in 2010? Does the present, or the immediate future, preoccupy you? Do you think about it?

François Mitterrand: No. Willy Brandt had this lovely phrase inscribed on his tombstone, and I will say the same: "I did what I could do."